JACKSON ODENY OYOO

Memories of My Life

My human roots and the Paradigm Shift to God's Kingdom

TABLE OF CONTENTS

Jackson Odeny Oyoo;   Memories of my life.

Jackson Odeny Oyoo;   Memories of my life.

DEDICATION

This book is dedicated to the Lord of my life, Jesus Christ. He remains the corner stone upon which I am building my whole life.

PREFACE

It is almost fifty eight years since my father died, forty years since I graduated from university and two years since I retired from active formal employment. Rounding up all these years brings me to ask myself some questions about my human roots for which I have no clear answers, but answers based on stories from my late fore fathers. Some of the answers are also based on sketchy information I received from the people above my age bracket whom I interacted with and who in the least knew how to read and write.

I remember sitting down and hearing stories, in the 1970's and 1980's, from my old kinsmen uncles; the late Eliazaro Otimo, the late Christopher Omolo, the late Were Muom, the late Nashon Owuocha, the late Amos Ochong' and my old mothers; My blood mother the late Jane Anyango Oyoo and the late Yunia Owaga Otimo. There were also people who went to higher levels of schooling in their time like Christopher Ojienda Odayo one of the pioneer graduates of education with vast knowledge on Gem Rae roots; James Audo Were, a pioneer statistician who authored a book on *'Jieyi gi De nyar ode'* and Isaiah Oloo, a painter also with

Jackson Odeny Oyoo;   Memories of my life.

ample knowledge on Gem Rae roots. These men of reputation put what they heard or read on pen and paper.

All these became integral information upon which I built the story of my origins. The information, though scanty, was useful enough to make me establish the pattern of my ancestral roots.

There were the tap root and the lateral roots of our history which enabled me to come on with my own summary, for which I am indeed proud and take full responsibility. I came to the conclusion that my tap root, my first known ancestor was known as **Luo Ganda**. Luo Ganda in my direct ancestral line moves down as follows:

MY ROOTS

(1ST TO 17TH GENERATION)

17th GENERATIONN – LUO GANDA

16TH GENATIION – PODHO KOMA

15TH GENATIION – LUO

14TH GENATIION – JOK

Jackson Odeny Oyoo;   Memories of my life.

13TH GENATIION – RAMOGI

12TH GENATIION – RAMOGI AJWANG'

11TH GENATIION – OCHIELO

10TH GENATIION – RAGEMA

9TH GENATIION – KWENDA

8TH GENATIION – OJUODHI

7TH GENATIION – THOMO

6TH GENATIION – NYANGLA OREMO

5TH GENATIION – OSANO AJWANG

4TH GENATIION – OYOO

3RD GENATIION – OLOO

2ND GENERATION – ZAKAYO JABUYA

1ST GENERATION – EDWARD OYOO

STARTING GENERATION – JACKSON ODENY OYOO

I see in the above a long genealogy of my roots, 17 generations in total. This is as far as I heard from the narratives of my forefathers and read from history books.

 This genealogy has helped me to tear down into my life and come to the rude awakening that what I am has been shaped by where I come from, built over many generations from my father Edward Oyoo to Luo Ganda, my great great grandfather. So here I am, with a character embedded from different underlying circumstances, some of which I am responsible for, but some emanating from many generations before me. I have elaborated on my human roots in the last chapter of part one of this book.

A person who comes from such a background is heir to imprecations that may be compared to weeds planted in his life, linking him to dark supernatural forces outside himself. This weed has two kinds of roots: one long tap root going straight downward, and other less powerful lateral roots stretching out in various directions. The tap root represents the influence of ancestors who may have worshiped false gods. Usually the taproot may entrench through the whole fabric of the clan or Community as a whole and may have cut across generations. The lateral roots are the other influences

Jackson Odeny Oyoo;   Memories of my life.

to which the person has been exposed in his own lifetime, either through acts of commission or through acts of omission, depending on the prevailing circumstances of the moment. The two types of roots integrate to form the character of the individual. This was the basis of my character flaws.

But I discovered that my ancestral roots limit me as to my total being or my whole heritage. As a matter of fact the roots only helped me to identify the idiosyncrasies in my life and to know that I am a subject of limitations if I refuse to recognize that I owe my total being to a higher power without limits. I fully acknowledged the identity of my whole self with the divine nature of my lord and savior, Jesus Christ. I accepted his mentorship, having escaped the putridity of the world brought about by my carnal heritage. I am building a story about my identity in the world and about my identity in the Kingdom of God.

Life is full of memories. Every time I pause to go to sleep or to wake up before my morning prayers I let my mind to be free, and my head starts to be full of different images, peoples, places, events; experiences that have left an indelible mark in my life. Sometimes these memories are happy, but other times they fill me with sadness.

Despite making me happy or sad, they have had great value, for they have always reenergized me to remain steadfast in my walk with Christ. People would start thinking that I am weak when I talk about my glaring weaknesses, but it is in exposing them that I have managed to clear my conscience of my wrongdoings and to become strong as a result. I remain fully convinced that I can neither lean on my own understanding nor even in the vast knowledge I have acquired over the years. I will continue to lean on God, faithfully serving him and living according to his will.

I will share these memories in two different perspectives: one when I was always struggling with life, exposed to some of the best institutions of learning in this Country. I became an academic giant in my own right but struggled through many ups and downs of life, some so bitter, some so sweet. I travelled places, became exposed to different training institutions and different places of recreation. I met different people, who exposed me to good habits and bad habits. I continued searching and searching for what I call the

Jackson Odeny Oyoo; Memories of my life.

unknown. In the end I stopped searching when I discovered the secret of my emptiness.

Secondly, I do not want to show that I am weak, but these memories have helped me grow up and understand the value of life and the value of belonging. These memories have catapulted me to give God the first place in my life in all circumstances, whether good or bad. Unfortunately, I only understood the value of life when I went through my most difficult relational circumstances, the circumstances which shaped my life to be what I am today in Christ Jesus.

I have no regrets at all in living in the Kingdom of God, and I'll continue to do so, without any fear of contradiction, until I transit from this temporal body I am clothed in, to the higher eternal life inheritance which is my hope.

Jackson Odeny Oyoo;   Memories of my life.

Part one:

My

Worldly Life

CHAPTER 1

27TH APRIL 1963, THE BEGINNING OF TRANSITION.

Some memories never fade away with time. 27th April 1963 is more than five decades ago, but what happened that day is still as fresh in my mind as if it happened yesterday. A few months before that day I had, at a very tender age of seven years, swallowed some medicinal tablet which was meant for my sick father, who laid on his sick bed, oblivious of what was happening around him. I presume it was a malaria tablet, if not some medicine reminiscent of modern day bitter pills used in the treatment of malaria. I struggled with this bitterness in my mouth without telling my sister or mother up to the time I fell asleep against my desire. Indeed this was a rude awakening never to taste medicine adults take when they are sick. It was as if I was playing with death. The angels were, however on my side. I survived. This is one of the memories which never faded away from my unconscious mind.

The other memorable moment in our life with our father was during the times of going to sleep at night. I was the cheeky one, always stubborn and reluctant to go to bed. We used to

Jackson Odeny Oyoo;   Memories of my life.

sleep in a small wooden bed with two floors. My sister would be sleeping on the upper floor of the bed and I on the lower one. Unfortunately I hated going to sleep, preferring to be cajoled by my father until I faded away into deep sleep. On such stubborn occasions my father would just take me outside into the dark and leave me 'for the hyenas', as he claimed. Hyenas' cries were common those days, hence this was a matter of life and death. What i realize now is that he must have been watching me very jealously from a very safe distance, to ensure my safety as I underwent through the one minute punishment. To my parents this was the antidote for my stubbornness, though risky.

But the greatest moment came some several months, if not a year later, on 27th April 1963.

On this day, my father laid prostrate on his sick bed, unable to talk, but seemingly waiting for something, which in my thinking, was so precious to him, more than gold or silver. My mother and my sister were just there, panicking and waiting for the unimaginable to happen. There were great expectations. For my dad he was anxiously expecting his brother in law because he had something to tell him, despite being too weak for anything meaningful to come from his

Jackson Odeny Oyoo;   Memories of my life.

mouth. For my mother and sister, they were facing the reality of an imminent death of their only source of livelihood, my father. For me, I wonder whether I was expecting anything. Nothing mattered to me except for the excitements around the house.

Our house was a small grass thatched house consisting of two small rooms. The house, what we called home, consisted of one small bedroom and a small sitting room with a transistor radio, the most precious thing inside. Lest I forget, there was also a Humber bicycle which my father had bought some months earlier. He used the bicycle as his means of transport from home to Urudi primary school where he was teaching. There was also a sofa set which only teachers could afford. Teachers were the high class echelons of the village.

As for me the radio was most valuable and unique thing in the house, more valuable than even the bicycle. The radio looked like a tiny house containing people who were talking and playing music inside. I kept on wondering how these people got into this small thing with their music instruments. Where was the door and how did they all fit into this tiny thing compared even to my whole mass of body? This was a

Jackson Odeny Oyoo;   Memories of my life.

wonder of wonders. The memories of those moments remained photographic in my mind up to now.

The moment of truth arrived like lightning. One of my maternal uncles whom my father had been expecting arrived. To be sure he was expecting both of them, the elder one Hezbon Manoa Omolo and his younger brother, Jeconiah Nyagweth Achola. Hezbon was the first born in this family of my Maternal Grandfather Thaddayo Majanga,   followed by my Mother Jane Anyango Polo and Jeconiah as the third born. Only the younger brother, Jeconiah came. He was carrying a small bag and inside it contained his small utilities for the night and some medicine for my father. As he sat down, my father leaped from his bed and became agile, to the surprise of everyone. Some strength overtook his physical weakness and he started talking. He said something like this,

"Brother in law, why did you take long to arrive?

I have been waiting for you all these days, but I am happy you have come in good time to let you know what I have in mind. If it were that I was not waiting for you, I would have faded off long time ago.

Jackson Odeny Oyoo;   Memories of my life.

This is why I needed both of you.

This disease, the cause which I am unable to explain, has eaten into a greater part of my strength. It has overtaken me and I am about to leave this world.

But one thing which has been worrying me and at the same time giving me strength me to move on, is the condition under which I am going to leave my children.

I know in our home here, nobody has the capacity, let alone the will to take care of them.

I am pleading with you, my brothers in law, that you take the responsibility of bringing up the first two, Alice and Odeny.

Please take care of them, kindly pay for their school fees and ensure that they live to their full capacity.

They will take care of the others when they grow up.

I am more mentally pained than this physical pain, to come to terms with this fact that I am leaving them to be domestic workers for other people because of my coming imminent death.

Jackson Odeny Oyoo;   Memories of my life.

How wretched I am as I lose control of my every desire ...”

Then there was silence followed by a sharp cry and a last grasp of air from the hero I had known all the days of my short life on earth. With those last words, my father's soul left him.

This was the close of one chapter in our lives.

With the close of the chapter came the burial plans. I remember my late uncle Jonam Akowa bringing a coffin for the burial and a wooden cross which was inscribed the following words:

Edward Oyoo

Died 27th April 1963.

On the day of burial, I saw my sister walking in with my maternal grandmother from outside the home. They seemed to have come all the way from Kabar, my maternal grandmother's home, I ran to welcome them very happily and laughingly told my sister, “ *Alice owada babawa otho”*, oblivious of the wilderness future which awaited us.

Jackson Odeny Oyoo;   Memories of my life.

One thing which confuses me is the memory that my sister was there when my father died while at the subsequent moment I see her arriving from somewhere with my maternal grandmother on the day of the burial. I am not sure what happened, but let's have it that she was around on both occasions. Then a group of people in white robs led by their leader Ammon Arach came. They were singing Christian songs and beating drums, something like drums of war. Nevertheless they undertook the burial ceremony in great style. The men in this congregation wore white hats inscribed 'ISRAEL'

What bewildered me was why my father was buried by these Israel Nineveh denomination people, while we used to fellowship with him at the local Anglican Church. Why didn't the Anglican Church participate in his burial plans?

 By the way I was a great darling of my father. He loved me dearly and walked with me everywhere he went. I remember him travelling with me to Miwani sugar Mills where I had the opportunity to see the factory. I had never seen such a wonderful environment. It looked like paradise. I also remember him making for me a car with clay and four wheels. In the evening, after playing or driving 'my car' I hid

Jackson Odeny Oyoo; Memories of my life.

it behind the sofa set in our sitting room and somehow never slept the whole night thinking of the great day ahead which awaited me with my 'car'. To my greatest disappointment of that moment, my mother had damaged the car beyond repair, I presume when she was sweeping the room. I never forgave her as far as I can remember but mourned over the loss over a very long period.

Later on after some time, I asked my mother why The Anglican church did not participate in the burial ceremony of my father, despite being a member of the church. Her reply was indeed very simple yet astonishing. She said this could not happen because we allowed our father to be treated by traditional doctors and this was against the Anglican faith. This being a shock to her as she never expected the church to follow this path, she decided to leave the Anglican faith for good. Indeed she never went back to fellowship with the church until her death in 2013.

The subsequent months rolled without anything worth of memory except for two occasions; one, when I and my sister were fighting over a living snake, which had crawled into our house. We fought over the snake, unaware that we were exposing our lives to grave danger. Alice had the head and I had the tail. To us it was just a toy to play around with. Luckily Samuel Oyare, now in his prime old age, came to our rescue and separated us from the snake.

The second thing which bewildered me were the times when there were struggles between my mother and my uncles, over small things. Or could they be big things in their perception? Well, they were struggles over small inheritances that our father had left behind; the bicycle, the watch, the clothes, the utensils etc. But one stood out clearly, when the small house our father left for us was pulled down by one of the uncles. We were thrown into the wilderness and my mother took us for refuge to their home at Kabar.

My first uncle, Hezbon, being the strong personality he was, brought us back with an unequivocal message to my paternal uncles never to play with their sister. There was nowhere she was going to go with Oyoo's four children. With that came the breath of life for my mother and her four children. An iron roofed house was built for her outside the original grandfather's home. That's how she managed to stay in Gem Rae until her death in 2013, fifty years after the death of my father.

Jackson Odeny Oyoo;   Memories of my life.

Despite these challenges, there were also times of momentary happiness and excitement for the children of the village. Gem Rae was a small sleeping village, nothing of color. During these earlier years there was one vehicle only and not more than three bicycles including the one of my father. The pickup vehicle belonged to one Elijah Kato who later on migrated to South Nyanza presumably for greener pastures. What made the village exciting was this vehicle. It was always stuck in the mud on the way to their home along River Awach swamps. During such times villagers would gather around to push the vehicle and all the children in the village would follow the vehicle with ululations. Some of the children in my age bracket included Jared Oloo Ombwa (deceased), Auma Rieko (deceased), Ajwang Ndia, Osano Ongudha, Otieno Ogada, Uko Awaa (deceased), Jomo Were, Olum Richard (deceased) and Jacob Akowa, These were our happy moments.

Then came the year of reckoning, 1964. When Schools closed, our Aunt, Joan Akoth, visited us from Kabar, our mother's home of birth. Little did we know that this visit would be a turning point in our lives. She had a simple message to deliver, that she had been sent by our grandmother to take us to Kabar, in pursuit of further education as per the wish of our late father. My aunt was a strong athletic lady. She had come all the way riding a bicycle, something which was very rare for women to do those days.

Nevertheless without any questions we set for the journey to Kabar the following day at 900 AM. We were carried this way; Alice at the back, Joan the rider in the middle and me in front. It was a long tedious journey with many challenges. We met our first challenge at Ahero, when the Police arrested us for using a bicycle without a *number,* presumably without a bicycle license. Bicycle licenses were yellow reflectors with numbers pasted on the hind mudguard. If one was caught without it, he or she had to pay a fine of Kshs 5. My aunt did not have this kind of money, so she was locked inside the *cell* (remand) while we remained outside.

As a matter of fact the police did not care about us, two hungry frightened children with visible looks of desperation. What I can remember is that she was released at around 5 PM and we had to continue with our journey from this time. The punishment given was to lock our aunt for five hours, in order to inflict utmost suffering for all of us. Indeed they succeeded in doing so. The weather was very bad, raining

Jackson Odeny Oyoo; Memories of my life.

throughout the evening with a very muddy terrain. We however had no alternative but to continue with the journey, most of the time walking because of the challenge of mud.

When we reached somewhere in the middle of the journey, a place called Ombeyi, we were forced to have an overnight stay at a relative's home because the night was approaching. In those days visitors were highly regarded by relatives, hence our stopover at the late Pastor Hezron Amolo's home was an enjoyment of warm reception punctuated with reflections about our struggle to reach there without any prior notice. In those days, such visits were done with prior notification in order to allow for meal plans and preparations. Nevertheless we were served with Ugali and chicken, the meal of honor for highly regarded visitors. I remember in this home there were two women; Wilkister Okuku, the mother of Jenifer, my maternal uncle's wife and her co-wife (*nyieke*) Peninah Ogwe, the wife of Dishon Ouma, Pastor Amolo's brother. These lovely women would impact my life in many special ways. I always visited them in later years.

The following day we embarked on the last part of our journey at 1000 AM reaching Kabar at around 1200 Noon.

And this marked the beginning of a ten year journey of life in

a distant land, the land of my mother's birth

Jackson Odeny Oyoo; Memories of my life.

CHAPTER 2

THE FIRST WILDERNESS EXPERIENCE: locating my bearing.

It all started with Nyakoko Primary School, where I and my sister Alice were admitted to begin our primary education from standard three. Alice was bright, always in position one at the end of each term. As for me, I was so naïve, to the extent that I didn't even know why I was going to school, always number twenty four in end term exams. I never knew of a person who was as cruel as my aunt, always beating us for trivial things. I always received my slaps during her coaching in the evening. In fact, I didn't understand whatever she taught me. It was just like a passing wind. I later on came to know the cause of my naivety. It was because of the beatings I received into my confused empty head which yielded no positive results.

The headmaster of the school was one Abednego Nam, who in the later years rose through the ladder of the Ministry of education to become a top officer. He is still alive and I recognize him very well. Unfortunately he doesn't know, let alone recognize me. He however did a good job in the school, at curriculum level and in extracurricular activities. Indeed

Jackson Odeny Oyoo;   Memories of my life.

because of his extraordinary performance, Nyakoko Primary School always emerged the best in sports.

One thing which pleased me with my aunt was that she was an extraordinary lady when it came to sports, always emerging number one in 100 meters race. She would always scoop the cup of 100 meters up to Provincial level. I was later told she became friends with a fellow sportsman who would later become her husband, because of sports ties. Samuel Sande was always number one in 100 meters like her. They psychologically bonded together through sports which ended up in a marriage in 1966. I have never forgotten what an exciting life we had together with our Aunt in those two years before she left us for marriage.

Life at Nyakoko Primary School was exciting. We interacted with several teachers as time passed, among them the Headmasters who followed Mr. Nam like Mr.Elisha Owese Ombuor, Mr. Meshack Orieny, teachers like Mr. Paul Oduwo, Mr. Abeneah Adongo, Mr. Odari and Mr. Jonam Aluoch.

Each of these teachers had their distinguished characteristics, something unique, what modern day refers as gifts, talents and abilities. Elisha Owese was not only the

Jackson Odeny Oyoo;   Memories of my life.

Headmaster but a gifted singer. He led the School Choir. One of his songs in the native language was about Kabar inheritance. Some of the excerpts of the song were as follows

Kabar Kogola nokedo gi lang'o piny lich miwuoro
Kata Atieno wuon Okuoga nenoyiech ageng'a
Ei apidi piny lich miwuoro…….

This, loosely translated, is the story of the tribal wars between Kabar people and their neighbors, the Lang'o people in the old days, during which Atieno the father of Okuoga played a major role.

We sang our hearts out because we loved the song. Unfortunately Elisha's headship did not survive because of one grave mistake he was caught in. Despite collecting fees for registering Standard eight pupils for national examinations, he did not do the registration. This was only discovered on the day of the exams and Parents howled for his blood when they realized that their children had been disqualified from taking the exams. He escaped and migrated to some distant land within the country. We later found that he had escaped to South Nyanza and he never came back for

Jackson Odeny Oyoo;   Memories of my life.

the entire ten years that I spent in Kabar. Fortunately for him, Kabar people allowed him to bury his wife, Selah, who died many years later.

Meshack Orieny, the Headmaster after Elisha Owese excelled in music. He led us in the songs like *'They have taken her to Georgia. They have taken her Georgia for to toil in the soil and the cane. Oh my poor Nelly Grey, they have taken her away, and I'll never see her any more…'* which we sang up to Provincial level. My participation was in the soprano. Paul oduwo was a teacher of Kiswahili. My assessment was that he was teaching something which he did not understand in the first place. He had difficulty in speaking the language. Abeneah was a teacher of English and was fond of saying *'paadn' which* meant *pardon.* Up to now I do not comprehend why he loved this word all the time. The brightest of all these teachers were the last two, Mr. Odari and Mr. Jonam Aluoch, God save their souls. Both of the taught Mathematics. Mr. Odari was fond of writing *untidy* in the exercises books for the homeworks that he gave us.

The pattern of daily activity was such that every morning started with taking tea or porridge prepared by my grandmother. By the way, my grandmother took good care

Jackson Odeny Oyoo;   Memories of my life.

of us. I do not remember any day we went without food. We would every morning carry two or three sticks of firewood as per instruction received the previous day from the teacher on duty. We were keen not to be late for morning parade, for being late attracted two or three strokes of cane. Because of fear of the cane, I was always punctual. I wonder why I learnt from the cane and refused to learn from the beatings of my aunt. Nevertheless having been caned positive outcome formed part of my conviction that caning should never have been withdrawn from schools. It formed a serious part of the discipline process of a child.

The social activities in Kabar were quite interesting and full of joy. There was always an evening wrestling match between Kabar clan and their immediate neighboring clan, Wang'aya. Despite the fact that I was very young, I always found myself among the people who walked three kilometers to watch these wrestling matches at Kodhiambo boundary field (the boundary land between Wangaya and Kabar, similar to a no man's land).

One memorable occasion, reminiscent of David and Goliath battle in the Bible, was when Kabar produced their strong man Buore wuod Nyagoro and Wangaya produced their strongman Ong'wen. Buore was strongly built, a proud man in all respects, always neatly dressed with beautifully combed long hair. He was the darling and hero of Kabar on that day. On the other hand Ong'wen was short and stout, with strongly built bones. Similarly he was the darling and hero of Wang'aya people.

What was quite interesting was the display of the two men before the fight, with songs of ululation from each side. The scene was such that Kabar would carry their proposed hero of the match and walk him around the enemy territory with war songs mixed with drum beats. Wang'aya would similarly walk their hero along kabar territory ululating war songs and drum beats. It was quite an exciting scene to watch.

Then came the time of reckoning. What I saw that day is still fresh in my mind as if it happened yesterday. The two wrestlers, each proudly matched to the middle field unescorted and took alert positions similar to what Paul has written in Ephesians 6;13, thus ' therefore put on the full amour of God, so that when the day of evil comes, you may be able to stand your ground, and after you have done everything, to stand'. After doing everything for alertness, each wrestler stood his ground. It was around 500 PM.

Jackson Odeny Oyoo;   Memories of my life.

I wish one was there to see what happened that evening. Within a flash of a second Ong'wen lifted Buore up and brought him down with a lightning thud. It was finished. Wang'aya people took their hero wrestler and proudly displayed him in the enemy territory. Kabar people were beaten to a dumbness never imagined before by them. That was real defeat. The scene has never left my memory, even fifty five years later.

Living in Kabar had also its fears. One challenge which readily comes to fore was the fear of night runners. At night one would just strike to instill fear among the villagers. One particular night runner which was well known was a Mr. Kola, who has now grown old and has since reformed. He would strike at around midnight and hurl stones on our grandmother's iron roof. This would instill great fear among us, grandmother included.

We also had our distant uncle Ongoyi who was a real terror to us .His activities were, however, in broad daylight. He would strike in the day and cause horror to my Grandmother and us children by extension. For instance there was a day, during hour, when he snatched from the dining table the whole plate of ugali and ran away with it, leaving us in

Jackson Odeny Oyoo;   Memories of my life.

amazement. He continued with this character until his death in the 1990's. He was buried homeless and landless after selling all his potions and sending away all his wives, including the last loving one, Pascalia. He was buried with a few people, similar to Anania and Safira's burial of the Bible. The burial ground was a donation of Hezbon's potion of land.

Meanwhile in the latter years, I found myself in the company of my first cousins who had joined me to stay with our grandmother. Their coming was for different reasons.

The sons of Jeconiah, I believe, were brought into the scene because their mother Julian Nakamya, who was a Ugandan, differed with their father and went back to Uganda. The father didn't have any option except to bring his children under the care of his mother. They were John Majanga (deceased), Patrick Tina Lumumba (deceased) and Sanyo Achola.

 The children of Hezbon came just because their father wanted them to have a taste of rural life. There was also the issue of polygamy as their father had taken a second wife by the nick name Nyanyakach. Hezbon's children were children were Loyce Akinyi, Simon Kungu, Nerry Otieno and Eucabeth

Jackson Odeny Oyoo; Memories of my life.

Awino. They did not all arrive at the same time. Loyce came first, followed by the rest. Their mother Jenifer Dola later joined us in 1968 to permanently stay at home until her premature death in 1974.

By virtue of my age, being the older one, I automatically became the leader of this group of children in a very informal way. I ensured that they took their berths in the evening and had their home works done after dinner. Of course sometimes I met with a lot of resistance in this leadership role. John who was next in terms of age was an entertainer and always made people laugh heartily. He always avoided responsibility through cheeky means. Sometimes I would find myself in physical fights with him. Lumumba the follower was tough and always never bent low to any of my directions. We however went along well as he carried himself with some respect.

Loyce was the darling of my grandmother. My grandmother always covered her mistakes even when they were glaring. My relationship with Loyce was a mixture of like and resentment. The resentment aspect was because of the soft attitude my grandmother had for her even when she committed certain mistakes which in my perception called

Jackson Odeny Oyoo;   Memories of my life.

for thorough beatings, like she always did to me. For me any mistake committed called for a thorough beating.

Unknown to both my granny and Loyce, I also made Loyce a ransom for my mistakes. One day I 'stole' the family bicycle and had a small accident which resulted into the breaking of the pedal from the riding arm. The rule was that nobody was supposed to play with the bicycle unless one wanted a thorough beating from granny. Indeed these beatings had been meted on me whenever I broke this rule. But this day I was the unlucky one. I had to craft a way out, lest I end up with a punishment. Previously I had always 'stolen' the bicycle without notice.

Knowing very well the consequences of this unfortunate incident, I decided to sell out Loyce as a ransom. I took the broken pedal and tied it to the arm using a small string. The idea was to pretentiously call Loyce and cheat her into a small ride with my assistance, for the purpose of shifting responsibility for the damage. It worked. She agreed and the pedal immediately broke off from the arm as she tried to ride. Immediately this evil mission was accomplished, I started shouting around, that Loyce had broken the pedal,

Jackson Odeny Oyoo;   Memories of my life.

until my granny came back from some small errand she was undertaking.

Unfortunately against my expectation, she did not receive any punishment apart from being told not to repeat such a mistake. Such were the causes of my resentment for her. But inside me I knew I had made her a ransom for my mistake. This remained my secret as I never told anybody.

Loyce was a very bright child, the reason she passed all exams at every stage and ended up with *Phd* in the sciences. In later years we were bonded together through emotional links brought about by the foundational struggles and the commotions in our youthful years and the subsequent successes we achieved in the field of education. Loyce followed my footsteps in education and surpassed me, for she went beyond the first degree, the maximum formal level I achieved in education.

Simeon was a humble and very generous boy. He would, however, always craft a revenge mission after every discipline he received from me, sometimes with success. I remember one day he made a mistake and I decided to discipline him. After dispensing my discipline we continued with our normal daily activities, only to realize later that he had a revenge mission in his heart. I just felt a sting of a small stone hitting my head from a safe distance. Having accomplished his mission, he walked away broadly smiling and happy, satisfied that his revenge mission was fulfilled. He ended up as Banker with The Central Bank of Kenya.

Nerry was a humble, non-controversial boy, always decent in behavior. I think this astuteness of character is what later earned him a place among the doctors roll in Kenya. He ended up studying medicine at Nairobi University and is now known as Dr. Nerry Omollo and practices in one of the countries in Southern Africa. Some other cousins who came along the way included Eucabeth Awino, Ammon Onyango, Paul Genga and Juma Achola . My association with them during this period was however brief, but I have some memorable moments concerning some of them.

For Juma Achola whose mother was Florence, nicknamed Nyalego, the night he was born comes vividly into my memory. He made a loud cry which we heard in the house where we were anxiously waiting for the good news. This was around 1965 or so. For Paul Genga I remember her mother carrying him, a brand new baby from Kisumu Shabir Hospital.

Jackson Odeny Oyoo;   Memories of my life.

No wonder he was nicknamed Shabir, a name which he dropped, or did it fade away in later years? This was around 1969 or so.

We also had interactions with these other cousins, my distant cousin Sarah Omia who hailed from Asembo and the other first cousin Janet Adhiambo who hailed from Kabonyo. All of us came here because of lack, in terms of support for education specifically and poverty in general. Adhiambo was tough headed and would sometimes fast without food for up to one week when annoyed by anybody in the home. Sarah liked to eat a lot and this behavior was an everyday complaint from my grandmother.

All of us, more than five children, used to sleep in a mat spread over the sitting room of my grandmother. During the night before sleep our grandmother would tell us stories. In the mornings she would always pray the morning as narrated in the New Testament Bible. My grandmother was a fervent lover of the word of God. She would always take us to the local *hera* where we would attend the children service handled by an elder called Killion Magaga. Killion inspired us. We adored him. I was later told this church was demolished because of land issues.

Jackson Odeny Oyoo;   Memories of my life.

Life in Kabar was not all roses. During our free times when not in school, all of us would be engaged in sugar plantation activities from 6 00 AM to 1 00 PM without touching any meals, whether breakfast or lunch. Those who worked below the desired measured level were not supposed to eat. They would forgo the next meal as severe punishment. I learnt over the years that this strict discipline meted to us shaped my later life.

Indeed my Religious Education Teacher, Namaan Abira later on taught us about what Paul said in the New Testament book of first Thessalonians 4, 11- 12 which read *"Make it your ambition to lead a quiet life. You should mind your own business and work with your hands, just as we told you, so that your daily life may win the respect of outsiders and so that you will not be dependent on anybody"*. This was taught together with second Thessalonians 3; 7-10, thus, "For *you know yourselves how you ought to imitate us. For we behaved not ourselves disorderly among you. Neither did we eat bread for naught, but in labor and travail, working night and day, that we might not burden any of you. Not because we have not the right, but to make ourselves an example to you, that you should imitate us. For even when we were with*

Jackson Odeny Oyoo;   Memories of my life.

you, this we commanded you, if any will not work, neither let him eat."

One thing which surprised us with our grandmother was that despite not having received any formal education, she knew how to read the Bible. Such relevant verses concerning work as read in the book of Thessalonians and righteousness as taught by Jesus in the Sermon on the Mount in the book of Mathews Chapter 5 were read to us almost every day after dinner.

In the overall what bound us together with my maternal cousins was fervent love and patience. We understood one another and this withstood the test of time. We still continue to meet and carry each other's burdens in seasons of lows and highs.

Something about my grandmother, the late Rosa Akanda Majanga. As a matter of knowledge I have never come across a woman as hardworking, witty and intelligent as my late maternal grandmother. Tough yet humble, she brought us up through high standards of discipline, hard work and honesty blended with humility. I only came to the realization of these qualities in my grandmother later on in life. May the Lord rest her soul in Eternal Peace.

More so, my two Uncles Hezbon Manoah omollo and Jeconiah Nyagweth Achola were epitomes of success in the village. They were better off compared to the other villagers during these earlier days. Both were driving their personal cars; Hezbon his Peugeot 205 old model registration KDA 105, and Jeconiah his Opel Kadett registration ARB 177. These were no mean achievements in the 1960's through to 1970's.

Back to school in the 1960's. After hobnobbing with age mates, some above me for two years or so, I gradually pulled out of my naivety situation, this only after repeating standard four class. I suddenly became bright and found myself in the first top five positions in every end term exam. This was a miracle.

Sometimes I ask myself whether the past foolishness was wrought by the beatings I used to receive from my aunt, or whether it was just natural stupidity. I ask so because I became bright after my aunt had left for marriage. Yes, I am

Jackson Odeny Oyoo;   Memories of my life.

convinced I was catapulted into being a fool by the frustrations I received.

Meanwhile my sister, being the person who could not bend low to mischievous behavior, took back to our home in Gem Rae where she finished the rest of her primary education. How she went back has faded out of my memory. As for me I became an agent of endurance which paid out handsomely at the end of my primary education. I emerged top in class and would thereafter proceed to Miwani Secondary School for my secondary education. The School was five kilometers away and I would be travelling to the school every day on foot the first one year.

I always visited my mother and siblings in Gem Rae during the school holidays during my primary school days. These visits usually happened in the months of April or August or December. The enthusiasm with which I waited for the d- day of the journey was usually beyond comprehension. A day prior to the visit, I would make all important preparations which included washing and ironing my clothes. It was only during this occasion that I ironed my clothes. In any case I did not know how to iron the clothes, even though I tried to.

The reason behind this was that I needed to look different among my peer groups in my village, to make an impression that I was better off than them. But inwardly I knew I was not any better, I had lost self-confidence, like most orphans, because of the loss of my father. I had been taken captive for the rescue of my life just like any other poor orphan would. Furthermore I enjoyed the advantage of a mother's love. To me my grandmother and my auntie were cruel people who enjoyed mistreating me under the pretext of discipline and giving direction. Hence going to visit my mother was great relief.

In the morning the laborer engaged by my uncles to take care of the home and the farms, Jectone Ombara Kola, would carry me with the family bicycle and take me to our paternal village. The journeys would start very early in the morning because they were meant to be return journeys. Two memorable incidents during these journeys flush into my mind;

One morning, on such a journey, Jectone nearly met with death. As he was riding the bicycle with me carried behind, a snake suddenly crawled and jumped into his gumboot. His quick instinct saved him as he threw himself out the bicycle

Jackson Odeny Oyoo;   Memories of my life.

with speed, leaving me juggling with the bicycle. Although he dislocated his knee in the process, he was safe.

Lest I forget, I was taken in my return journeys to Kabar by my elder cousin, Manuel Ombayi who would use another bicycle borrowed from my uncle Eliazaro Otimo. The return journeys were not as exciting as the journeys from Kabar to Rae. I didn't enjoy them. They was to me, like going back to hell, considering the frustrations I used to receive from my Aunt.

 In one morning incident, as we approached our home from Kabar with Jectone carrying me with the bicycle, my young brother and sister ran towards us in excitement and greeted Jectone with these words ' *Ombara wuod Kola, lake otop'* meaning '*Ombara son of Kola, his teeth are rotten*'. I recalled when coaching my cousins I wrote the same words in my native language and asked them to cite them loudly. Little did I know that this information was already in the domain of my siblings in Gem Rae, and that we would be greeted with such colloquial words! Quite interesting?

The holidays at my home village were quite exciting and enjoyable. My mother was always soft on me, the loving mother she was and kinder than my aunt and granny. She did not mind my frequent short absences from home, visiting my friends and just walking about. During August holidays we would organize tea parties and invite friends from the neighboring locations. Such parties would go throughout the night without any ugly incidents. Life in the village during such occasions were meant for joy, nothing else. We would dance ourselves out during the night and sleep undisturbed the following day. Two village mates stood out as excellent organizers of such parties, Hanningtone Uko Awaa and Jared Oloo Ombwa, God save their souls.

One memorable time with my paternal cousins during the school holidays: Somehow, we were emotionally attached to our elder most cousin Abigael Odongo who later married Samuel Nyanganga of Uyoma Katweng'a. Abigael would always lead the way in everything. One day she took us to swim at a nearby river Awach which nearly ended in a tragedy. I do not clearly remember what happened, but what comes to my mind is that I suddenly started drowning and the other cousins just stood helplessly on the side of the river, watching as I gulped the water. I ended up rescuing

Jackson Odeny Oyoo;   Memories of my life.

myself in a miraculous way when my stomach was full to the maximum.

One interesting about Abigael when she had already been married to the love of her life, she always came back during the August holidays with a Record Player. In those days there was no electricity, so the record players were run on dry battery cells. These were very happy moments as we would sit the whole day listening to luo music mixed with some English lyrics. We memorized everything that was sang. I remember my favourites were the ones of Musician George Ramogi such as *Conny dhi school Asumbi, Ajali ya Sondu, Rapar mar Tom Mboya and Opiyo Timmy ja Kabar.* Next on the line were Owino Misiani's records such as *Arusi ya MK, Ja nawi madhako Isabella, kech marauma biro* and *Amin Jamadar bol bunde piny iringi.* Then there were English lyrics of Jim Reeves such as; *this world is not my home* and *precious memories.*

The unfortunate thing was that Abigael stayed with her husband for nearly ten years without a child. Somehow God remembered her along the way and she bore Samuel a child followed by some others in later years. Samuel was a very loving husband. He extended that love to all of us. He would always visit us with a lot of goodies. Indeed this love became consummated when he built Abigael's parents a beautiful iron roofed house. In those days iron roofed houses were very rare and precious, except for a few homes.

My first woolen blanket was bought by my brother in law Samuel Nyanganga. Samuel sent me Shs.40, by means I cannot recall, to buy the blanket. I remember giving this money to my elder kinsman who was working as a supervisor at Great Oroba farm, some four kilometers away, to go and buy for me the blanket at Kisumu. What a great mistake I made, for I had to follow up this blanket for a period of more than three months. Every weekend I was in his house asking for my blanked, until he got tired with my persistence. In the end he bought the blanket, a great relief because of the cold weather at night in Kabar village. To me, this was the most precious property I owned.

My return journeys to Kabar at the close of school holidays were always full of disillusionment. I always felt like somebody going back to jail, because of the perceived frustrations from my grandmother and some distant uncles who used to jokingly refer to me as *'nyathi nyagwowa'*, loosely translated as *'the child of our dog'*. Nevertheless

Jackson Odeny Oyoo; Memories of my life.

there were also times of momentary happiness brought about by my paternal grandmother who always bid me bye by clinching one shilling into my hands accompanied with a strict remark ' do not tell your mother'. I would use this money to buy *mandazi* on the way to Kabar. As customary Jectone always came to collect me at the close of the holidays.

I joined Miwani Secondary School in January 1971, a journey of life which I would travel for the next four years. This journey was tough. I had no alternative but to go through it. I made a covenant with my heart not to disappoint my uncles who offered to pay my school fees. This offer was of course tied with the commitment they had undertaken with my late father on his deathbed, not to leave us behind on matters of education.

During the first one and half years, I walked a total of 10 kilometers (return journey) every day to go to the school and back. To me it was not tiring because my zeal and quest for education was higher than the tiring journey. When I had reached form two my uncle gave me his bicycle to help me with travel to school. This was quite a relief as it lifted off all the exhaustion I experienced in travelling on foot 10 kilometers daily. I would cycle for the rest of the year before the school was transformed into a Boarding School.

Of all the teachers who inspired my life, none can be compared to our Headmaster at Miwani secondary School, Mr, Remgius Rachiedo Ondeng'. The zeal with which he taught the Science subject of Biology, his mastery of English language, commitment to Physical education and training, the pride and compassion with which he held all the students, became reflected in all our life dispositions. He was the epitome of success, an excellence of character building and a propeller of inspiration. He surprised famous schools in Nyanza when he propelled the first Form Four class to excellent performance in National Exams, similarly followed with our class of form fours. Indeed I achieved top performance in my class because of his inspiration. I owe the pillars upon which I have built my life to him i.e. Inspiration, Focus, Determination and Passion.

Mr. Okoth Odaga taught us English. Two books which featured in his teachings were *Ongundipe's English learning book* and *The Animal Farm by George Orwell*. Mr. Okoth was very smart in his appearance, always expensively dressed with an omega watch in his right hand. He led us into a chorus

Jackson Odeny Oyoo;   Memories of my life.

'four legs good, two legs better', from the book of Animal Farm.

One memorable moment with Mr. Okoth Odaga is when he took as, Form ones and Form twos, on a picnic to the top of Nandi Hills, walking on foot all the way, a distance of more than five Kilometers one way. We did not have any security accompanying us, and the people living here were not bothered at all with our presence. As a matter of fact they seemed to have hidden in their houses, watching us from a safe distance. Nevertheless we had a good picnic and amusedly watched the rolling Kano Plains from the top of the hill. It was quite a beautiful scene to behold.

Mr. Ondeng' and Mr. Odaga were the only teachers of colour during my period at Miwani. Of course there were other teachers like Moses Abira, who taught Religious Education and Mr. Olero who taught Kiswahili. They also created an impact, but not as Mr. Ondeng and Mr. Odaga.

Student life at Miwani was quite exciting. We spent the first year as day scholars arriving at the school at 730 every morning and departing every 5 PM after games. In the evenings those who had bicycles like me were engaged in

Jackson Odeny Oyoo;   Memories of my life.

bicycle competition when going back home. It was tough. I was always at the tail end, being younger than my competitors.

I was also not much of a sportsperson as I used to dodge sports during game time. However, the sporting character of our headmaster energized even the weak ones like me. In class I excelled, always on top position in end term exams. I had two competitors for top position, Amos Akumu and Godfrey Otieno, God save their souls.

The greatest moments came during lunch hours. Majority of us came from poor backgrounds, hence could neither afford breakfast nor lunch. Those who afforded breakfast would go to a nearby market place called Karunga and take cooked maize and beans (*nyoyo*). A plate cost Two Shillings, quite valuable those days. Those of us who could not afford such meals hid in the nearby sugar plantations and chewed sugarcane to the full as lunch.

In our third year, we started to board at the school. This was another phase with fun and nightmares. I remember one night when we had gone to sleep and right in the middle of the dark a student would shout with a sharp feminine voice

Jackson Odeny Oyoo;   Memories of my life.

in an abusing language, " *Kisa, Kisa, lake otop*" , meaning " *Kisa, Kisa, your teeth are rotten*". We all knew it was Jared Onyango, the funny classmate whose bed was near mine. Kisa was a strong, muscular student whom nobody would dare face physically in broad daylight. He was always faced squarely in the dark at night with a small voice, for the purpose of hiding identity, lest you face him physically if discovered. This occasionally occurred when people had begun to fall asleep.

CHAPTER 3

ON THE WAY TO TOP ACADEMIC ACHIEVEMENTS

1974 was the year that would define my fate in later years. Unfortunately, it was not the year without misfortunes and challenges.

First I was stricken with a sickness which almost made me mad. I was admitted in Lake Nursing home with the admission card of my first cousin, Simeon Kungu. This was because whereas he enjoyed the benefits of National Hospital Insurance Fund by virtue of his father's employment at the then East African Railways and Harbors Corporation, I did not. If it were not because of this card, cerebral malaria would have taken my life prematurely. Although impersonation using such a card was against the rules of the Fund, all of us didn't care was because my life was on the line, sand there existed no rescue alternative

It all started during the August holidays at our home in Gem Rae. This was the year of my secondary National Exams, The East African Secondary Certificate of Education (E.A.S.C.E). As normal with preparations for exams of this magnitude, throughout the month of August, I was constantly indulged

Jackson Odeny Oyoo;   Memories of my life.

in revision work in the house we used for sleeping. It was also very normal to use neighbors houses for sleeping, the reason why we slept in Walter Odago's house, some 70 meters away. This fateful day, in the middle of the night, my head started to burst. It was a very terrible headache, hence my friend, whom we used to share the house with, Benson Otieno Ogada, rushed to our home call my mother.

Mother came and she didn't know how to handle this situation. During those days there were no nearby hospitals, let alone Doctors. So, she just sat there, crying and gazing at the roof. Apart from this she did not have even a single cent to facilitate her movements and there was nobody to ask. Nobody had money in the neighborhood.

 After gazing the whole night, only one idea came to her mind and this idea is what saved my life. She made up her mind to walk all the way on foot up to her home of birth, Kabar. She started very early in the morning and came back late afternoon with my uncle's wife, nicknamed 'Nyalego'. There was no time, it was a question of saving my life. So they rushed me to Kisumu using road transport which were also rare those days.

What I recall is that we ended up at Lake Nursing Home the following morning. I also recall spending that night in a distant relative's house who was very uncooperative. The relative was the brother to my paternal uncle's wife. Although he allowed me to sleep on the sofa set in his sitting room, he refused the same for my two mothers who had accompanied me to the house for night rescue. They were helpless. Up to now I do not even know where they slept.

I stayed At Lake Nursing Home for a long eighteen days, and left after being declared healed of cerebral malaria. When I went back to school I hardly had enough time to do my revision work. Nevertheless my Head Master insisted that despite the fact that I had been ill, I was still going to get Division one in my final exams. True to his prophesy I ended top of the class with a Division One achievement.

Then I lost my uncle's first wife, Jenifer Dola, who had been nicknamed 'Nyombeyi'. Nyombeyi had been a woman of grandeur in my life, always humble, welcoming and respectful. My greatest memory about her character comes out on the day I was doing my final primary school exams. She woke up to prepare for me a breakfast of my choice and gave it with an everlasting impression of love and hope. She

Jackson Odeny Oyoo; Memories of my life.

also did the same when I came back for lunch, after doing two papers.

In these exams there were three papers; English, Mathematics and General Paper. English and Mathematics papers were done in the morning and The General Paper was done in the afternoon after lunch. The lunch I was served was sumptuous, consisting of rice and chicken, a meal of the year. I believe this kingly treatment by my uncle's wife during this special occasion contributed immensely to my top achievement in these exams, earning me a place at a Government sponsored Secondary School.

There were two types of secondary School during this era: one was the type sponsored wholly by community members. They were called Harambee Schools. Majority of them lacked essential facilities and human resources required for good performance. They lacked chairs and desks, blackboards, trained teachers and facilitating workers. The net result was that they always performed poorly in national examinations.

On the other hand Government sponsored secondary schools had all these necessary facilities, which made them have a comparative advantage over Harambee schools. For one to be admitted to a government sponsored secondary school required comparative high performance. This is what I achieved and became proud of during this moment and later on in life. 1974 is the year that defined my fate, my life.

News about my top performance at Miwani came when I had gone to help my uncle with house cores in Nairobi. He had migrated all the members of his family consisting then of his first Jenifer (nyombeyi) with four children (loyce, Simeon, Nerry , Eucabeth and Paul and Omondi) and second wife Jane Agutu with one child (Allan) to permanently stay at home. He was then alone in Nairobi and frequently travelled to the rural home using his Peugeot 404 Registration number KHY 231.

On this great day, my Uncle arrived back from the rural home in the evening and as he alighted from his car he carried a piece of paper which I immediately recognized to be the result slip of my Examination results. As I read the results, I was overcome with a happiness I have never experienced in my life to date. I think there will never be such a moment until I reach heaven. In a moment, reflections and encapsulations about my past just came through my mind: the circumstances of the death of my father, our journey to

Jackson Odeny Oyoo;   Memories of my life.

Kabar in quest for education, our struggles in Kabar, my primary school days, my primary school results and now the end result of my secondary education. This was the distance I had reached. Surely my father's prayers had been answered. Division one in the results slip, unbelievable!

To me, I had achieved the epitome of my academic success and even the realization of other potential abilities. This was because success was majorly defined by the level of Form four examination results, nothing more. If one achieved top results, all doors of opportunities were opened: Free post-secondary trainings in the major fields of primary school teaching, human and animal health, agriculture and technical education. Formal jobs in Government Intuitions were guaranteed after one had acquired the necessary training. Those who excelled were admitted to higher levels of education, then known as 'A' level.

About four Kilometers away, within Nairobi, my sister Alice was also spending the after exam holidays with our Aunt Joan. Joan was, I believe, happily married to the love of her life Samuel Sande and they were working and earning their living in Nairobi; Joan as a primary school teacher and Samuel a retired Army Officer now working as an hotelier. They used

Jackson Odeny Oyoo;   Memories of my life.

to stay at Pangani before moving to Umoja. I walked all the way from Landi Mawe where I was staying with my Uncle to Pangani carrying the result slip in my hand, eager to deliver the good news to my sister.

Immediately I reached, we were all overtaken with joy. I learnt that Alice had also received her exam results and that she had equally emerged top of her class with a Division Two, thus opening her the doors to all opportunities. After celebrating our great success at Pangani I went back to my Landi Mawe residence fully satisfied that I had received a big favor in that my long sought for prayers had been answered. One funny thing i realize today is that despite having been taught Religious Studies during my secondary school and even in higher institutions of learning, I did not know God. I had no relationship with our Lord Jesus Christ. This is a matter which I really regretted later on in life, and which I intend to dwell on in the later chapters of this book.

At Landi Mawe my happiness was turned into awe because of a small mishap. A day earlier a neighbor from Kabar village had visited us in Nairobi en route to Mombasa in quest for a job. His name was Jairo son of Bita. Because he did not have enough money for the journey, he decided to come to the

Jackson Odeny Oyoo;   Memories of my life.

Landi Mawe residence for an overnight stay, in the hope of getting enough fare for the rest of the journey. With him was only a small bag which he was used in keeping the small utilities he had. He had also bought some new clothing and rubber shoes which I perceived to be the most precious belongings he had for his journey. At night he washed these belongings and hang them on a rope inside the verandah to let them dry overnight in readiness for the following day.

My uncle used to keep a very big German shepherd dog in the house. The house was large enough with a big verandah which accommodated the dog's kennel. Unknown to all of us the dog ate one shoe of Jairo's pair of shoes. This was a real tragedy because Jairo continued with his journey to Mombasa wearing one shoe on his left foot and no shoe on his right foot. I just wondered why he insisted he must wear the shoe on one foot and remain bare on the other foot because it looked awkward. My happiness was therefore mixed with the amazement of the moment. The incident kept on flushing into my mind up to this day.

Meanwhile celebrations about our exam results were going on at our home villages of Gem Rae and Kabar. During this moment of celebrations, my second Uncle Jeconiah, passed

Jackson Odeny Oyoo;   Memories of my life.

by Landi Mawe on his way to Arusha where he was working with the East African African Common Services Organization, later changed to East African Community. He was quite senior, holding the position of Senior Accountant. By Kabar standards he was the senior most civil servant in the region, driving a posh Toyota Corona Mark II, registration number KMU 714. He invited me to accompany him for a visit to Arusha, for the purpose of seeing the splendid beauty of Arusha with its magnificent trees, flowers, and buildings. I consented to this heartily and confirmed the stories he had telling me about Arusha when we arrived there in the evening. Suddenly I was at the center of attention and beautiful things. I started seeing the fruits of my academic success.

The only thing I didn't like about Arusha was the climate, being cold and rainy most times. I had grown up under hot weather conditions. My body disposition was therefore not compatible with this weather. Nevertheless I enjoyed the beauty of the environment, the welcoming nature of the people and seeing very beautiful women all around.

The people of Tanzania were, in my perception, more welcoming than Kenyan people, never in a hurry and always

Jackson Odeny Oyoo;   Memories of my life.

greeting whoever they came across with warm words of 'Shikamoo', with the replies ' *marahaba*'. If one wanted something from his or her colleague, the request was always with kind words '*naomba*'. This was the distinct difference I observed between the character of the people of Kenya and the people of Tanzania.

There were also very good musicians around Tengeru, the place we used to stay. Their music languages were always punctuated with sentimental words, like I remember one; 'Nategemea *jibu lako mwenzangu Hellena. Hellena njoo haraka tuishi pamoja'*; Very sentimental indeed during that time. Foreign volunteers also used to frequent Tengeru, one in particular being Danish Volunteers.

CHAPTER 4

CHOICES IN THE ACADEMIC LADDER

I and my sister were faced with making choices about our future.

For my sister it was already settled. Although she had passes which qualified her for High School admission. My mother had given the recommendation that she should cut short her education in order to train as a teacher. In my mother's view this would enable her to earn income in a shorter run for family support. She therefore went with the teacher training carrier option she had opted for while making her training choices. As per her wish she was called to train as a P1 Teacher at Kaimosi Training College in 1975. She went through this up to 1978, as she had some interruption of the birth of her first born child Judy Aseda, otherwise she would have completed in 1976.

Meanwhile midway through her college training she decided to marry somebody she had never introduced us to, indeed a complete stranger. I even took my time to go to Kaimosi to persuade her against this marriage, but her answer was a firm NO. I came back very disappointed. It took me long to come terms with this arrangement, but I let go in the long term. This was the beginning of a separation from a sister I had long held with respect, esteem and love.

As for me I had hard choices to make, either to proceed to high School or to go to a pilot training college. I was offered a Form Five chance at Kisii High School and an opportunity to train as a Pilot at Soroti Pilot Training School, Uganda. In those days, higher education was more precious than gold or silver, because education not only opened the doors of knowledge and wisdom but also the doors of innumerable opportunities. Whether one wanted to work, or to train any field more so the fields of education, agriculture and health were matters of choice. These were unlimited at every level of National Examination scores. They were freely received unlike the present days when such opportunities are majorly available through money influence.

The closest people in my life, the people who mattered in the direction which would later on define my life had different views. My mother insisted that I must continue with my education, saying that she had been used to struggling and she saw no reason to continue that way for a while as I pursued further education. My first uncle Hezbon insisted

Jackson Odeny Oyoo;   Memories of my life.

that I should look for work in order to carry the burden of my other brothers and sisters. My younger uncle was mixed up; He had already secured for me a place at a Pilot Training School in Uganda by virtue of being a senior Officer at the East African Common Services Organization. Here I was with two invitation letters, one for admission to Form Five at Kisii High School and the other for admission into a Pilot Training course at Soroti, Uganda. Both were pleasing to him. As for me I had no choice but to rely on their ultimate decision. My mother's desire carried the day. I went to Kisii High School to continue with further education.

My days at Kisii High school are also full of reflection. I had followed the footsteps of two somehow older friends who had become my mentors in a way. They inspired me to success in different ways, only known to me and not known to them. Phares Sumba was my senior at Miwani Secondary School. I admired the way he carried himself, dignified, hardworking and bright. He was a year my senior all throughout secondary to University. He excelled in Form four Examinations of 1973 with a Division one, scoring with distinctions in most of the subjects. This earned him a place to Kisii High School, the reason I selected Kisii as my preferred high school. He was later admitted to The University of Nairobi for a Bachelor of Commerce Degree, also the reason I chose Commerce as my preferred course. In secondary school, he was always smart and used to ride a bicycle he had been given by his brother who used to work at Railways at Miwani Railways Station, almost the same distance and place we travelled every day. He was always faster than me in the rides. I admired him, the reason he inspired my life.

Jecton Odhiambo Kiverenge was another inspiration of my life. His Waswa village neighbored my Gem Rae Village, but we shared the same market, Awach market, now extinct. Whenever we met, he was a great story teller, humorous and made all colleagues comfortable. Always smart in short trousers, he became my invisible friend because of his sharpness. I later learnt that he was always on top of his class in Secondary school, earning distinctions in the subjects he did in Form Four Exams. He also ended up at Nairobi University with a top honors Degree in Mechanical Engineering, We remained good friends up to the time of his death in November 2020. Whenever I went to Mombasa, his later place of residence, I always made sure to get accommodation in his high class Beaumont Hotel. I also admired his ways, the reason he was also my inspiration.

At Kisii High School I opted to take the subjects of History, Geography and Economics. It was interesting to meet my former school mates at Miwani, Apiyo and Phares who had joined one year earlier and were now in Form six. This was a national school of high standing in the Country. At that time high schools were graded into two types i.e. National and Provincial schools and I had passed well enough to be admitted in a national school.

There were more than five Dormitories with different house names. I can still remember Kuja House where I was staying, Wire, Kionganyo and Manga Houses. They used to compete against one another particularly in Sports and Drama. Kuja always took the lead position in Drama and being a member of this house we were always proud of this and even boasted about it.

The social classification of students were well defined. There were those who were visibly perceived to be in high class. They always flocked together in social gatherings. These were the students who could afford to prepare coffee using their private electric kettles and drink the coffee with buttered bread. Of course I found myself in the lower class strata, and all that we used to do was to watch them jealously from a safe distance. How would one dare to be near them when one did not have even a single cent in his pocket or private box? No, this was next to impossible. This team of people perceived to be highly placed included The Head masters children John and Dave, one Dick Dick, one Osewe and a handful of others

The interesting thing was that despite this group having the financial advantage, they were no match us in academic performance. We were giants when it came to end term examinations. Our inferior complexes were swallowed by academic performance, the basis of our confidence. We were overly hard working enough to secure ourselves a place at the two National Universities during this time, The University of Nairobi and Kenyatta University College which was a constituent college of the former. Some of us ended up with high caliber positions in the Government like Wycliffe Ambetsa Oparanya and Rasanga who became County Governors in their own rights.

At High school we envied our predecessors who had scored very high grades in the National Exams. Our best wish was to be like them. Indeed threir academic excellence endeared to high places either in the Government or in the private sector. Students like Nicolas Owano Ombija w became a Justice of the High Court of Kenya, Omondi Nandwa became a building economist of high standing, Pharesh Ratego became a minister in the County Government of Homabay. They were our invincible mentors in high School.

 At the end of our Form Six examinations the parting shot for one another was either 'See you at Karanja's place next year' or 'See you at the campus next year'. These two parting shots were synonymous with academic success and high motivation parameters in terms of working hard to ensure admission at the University. Dr. Karanja was then the vice Chancellor of Nairobi University. The name Campus was synonymous with success in life. We made it, all of us in the perceived lower social strata, to the University the following year as 'prophesized'.

Before entering Nairobi University I had a chance to work as untrained teacher at Kangaru High School, where I was placed to teach Geography in Form one class, thanks to the

Jackson Odeny Oyoo;   Memories of my life.

efforts of my neighbor at home Mr. Jasper Obaje who was then working at The Teachers' employer, The Teachers Service Commission. He had guided me through the process of applying for the job up to securing the job. He did it with a lot of enthusiasm.

In my own perception, I did not know how to teach, hence the form one students were always teasing me and calling me all sorts of names. Persistence however paid off as I ended up being a darling of the students as months rolled by. The Principal Mr. Njoka really assisted me to get me settled, providing me with all the necessities like a free fully furnished house, utensils and other utilities. I eternally thank him for coming to my rescue as I had gone to the school barehanded without anything at all. He even gave me small money to start me off.

It is at Kangaru that I was introduced the soft music of Jim Reeves, Don Williams, Charley Pride and Skeeter Davis. I really loved the songs 'You have to go', 'You have stay' by Jim Reeves and Skeeter Davies respectively. There was a stanza which I internalized in my heart, thus, 'once I loved you with my all my heart, but now I must say no. You broke my heart so many times... so now you have to go...'

Jackson Odeny Oyoo;   Memories of my life.

The teachers at Kangaru were equally cooperative. I was the youngest teacher, barely twenty one years old, teaching in a first class High School. We had teachers of national repute, most of them foreign teachers from Great Britain like Mr. Chadwick and Mr. Ram. I wonder whether they are still alive today. I had also Mr. Booker Onyango a fellow Luo teacher who was highly cooperative. He used to coach me how to go about teaching since I had not undergone any training in teaching. Mine was just a trial and error, thanks to Mr. Onyango who put me in the right track. Nevertheless all the teachers were a great inspiration in all fields including preparations before class, contributions in school meetings, contributions in school assemblies, recreations after classes etc.

My first salary came at the end of January 1977. It was accompanied with a pay slip with a net pay of KShs.800. I kept this slip for a very long time, up to the end of my university education as far as I can remember. Why, because it was so precious to me, tasting what I never thought would happen to my life. Sure to my heart, I did not waste this money but bought two beautiful dresses for my mother, which I would later take to her at the end of the school term. When I went

Jackson Odeny Oyoo;   Memories of my life.

back to the home village, I became a hero in my own right, an envy to my peers and a great joy to my mother.

I left Kangaru at the end of August 1977, ready to join the university the following month. At the time of registration I was faced with a small hiccup of getting Shs. 100.00 for the purpose of completing the registration process. When I requested the only cousin I knew in Nairobi he promised to avail it in the afternoon, only to disappear using the hind door when he saw me at the promised time. Looking for this money was a real struggle. Nevertheless a good Samaritan came to my rescue and I managed to complete the registration which enabled me to start the three year long journey of life within the University of Nairobi.

For me the challenges at Nairobi University were quite dissimilar from what I had faced in my Secondary and high Schools. I suddenly found myself in the middle of extreme academic giants who I were above me in terms performance. Most of them were from the top known High Schools like Alliance, Mangu, Kangaru and Maseno. Then there were the impatient lecturers who were never concerned with the absorption rate of students. They merely read their lecture notes, no questions, and period. I particularly remember

Professor Kariuki in accounts and Dr. Mukhwana in Marketing and Dr. Kwasa Kojudo in Economic Theory. But I also had my darling lectures like Prof Kamuntu in the subject of Quantitative Methods, Prof. Pherozee Nowrojee in Company law and Dr. Odada in Economic Theory.

Every week we had Continuous Assessment Tests (CATS) which paved way for End Term Examinations. Sometimes my dumb head could not respond effectively to some subject examinations at the end of the term. Quantitative Methods, and Cost Accounting were particularly bothersome. At one point, I thought of quitting the university altogether but persistence reigned over impatience. Some thoughts had reigned on my mind: First my village people had already known me as a very bright student. I thought they were not going to come to terms that I was now a great fool who could not finish his university education. This unshakeable reality made me to struggle very hard despite my shortcomings in performance. Persistence eventually prevailed. I was after all, not a fool as I progressively improved on my standards. In the end I enjoyed my class lessons and moved to higher echelons of academic performance.

Jackson Odeny Oyoo;   Memories of my life.

Then there were social interactions within the campus. At the Campus I found myself in endless freedom I had never known before, freedom of intellect, freedom of expression and freedom of going wherever I wanted. Here nobody bothered about what one did, whether you decided not to attend classes, or took your time visiting prostitutes, relatives or engaging in some other illicit activities in Nairobi. There was complete freedom of choice. But as the saying goes, choices had consequences.

During the first few months it is now clear to me that I made wrong choice of friends including where I spent my outings. I remember senior friends like the late Ouma Aboma who was doing land Economics and Odede who was doing Electrical Engineering, Ogwang Kohot and Otieno Okungu with whom we were in the Faculty of Commerce. All of them have since died or their lives went haywire except me and Kohot who surrendered their souls to Jesus Christ. These were no good people because they spent most of their times drinking alcohol in the city bars. I suddenly found myself in the company of these wrong people, spending my time drinking alcohol. The only luck on my side was that I was never involved in illicit drinks like 'chang'aa'. Be that as it was, I was in wrong companionships.

Being the outgoing students we were had also its advantages. Some of us had the advantage of working part time in our free times. I did get jobs to do during most of my lifespan at the University. First there was this business research work involving in sighting into the strengths and weaknesses of some selected financial institutions in Nairobi for which I was paid Shs. 1,000 per month; followed by working as a teller in Commercial Bank of Africa, Wabera Street for which I earned shs. 2,400 per month excluding overtime; and finally I got to work as a clerk in the Accounts and Finance Department of the then Kenya Posts and Telecommunications Corporation for which I earned Shs. 3,000. Probably the fact that we were money loaded most of the time could underscore the reason why we flocked together, that is me, Otieno Okungu, Tobias Ogwang Kohot and the others. Being paid handsomely at such a young age had its misgivings.

But what comes to fore in my mind is that I had suddenly forgotten the long road I had travelled in order to reach the university. If only I had known that it was the determination

Jackson Odeny Oyoo;   Memories of my life.

of my mother blended with the commitments of my maternal uncles, I shouldn't have travelled this road. The devil is a liar. It was only because of sheer good luck that I managed to complete my education. Young men and women should be very careful what companies they keep in the university, being the great freedom they enjoy upon admission. This freedom can mess a whole life.

On the other hand there were good mannered students whom I really envied. We had students like Otiende Ogara and Phares Ratego who were in the Christian fellowship Team, Ojwang Ogada, and Ambetsa Oparanya who carried themselves with high discipline. Mid way in between the two extremes were the likes of Bernad Mboha in BA class, the late Phillip Yogo and Peter Meyo in our class.

Riots were a common phenomenon in the University during our time. There were riots which were politically oriented, especially instigated to resist the government of the day when the University voice was dissenting. Such riots were led by the student leaders who in the majority of cases ended up expelled from the university. I can still remember the expulsion of my friend the late Otieno Okungu and the late Otieno Kajwang who were expelled because of leading a riot.

Jackson Odeny Oyoo;   Memories of my life.

They ended up completing their education at Makerere University. I also remember Lecturers who went on exile because of dissenting opinions like Professor Micere Mugo, Professor Ngungi Wa Thiong'o and Professor Anyang Nyong'o. The period 1977 to 1980 was a difficult time because dissenting voices were met with emphatic ruthlessness.

Nevertheless we managed to finish. I ended up with a Second Class Honors Degree in Bachelor of Commerce, Business Administration option, in 1980. To me this was no mean achievement, for it opened doors to great opportunities.

Jackson Odeny Oyoo;   Memories of my life.

CHAPTER 5

OUT INTO THE WORLD

19th December 1980 was our Graduation Day. This was great moment, for my mother and the younger wife of my maternal uncle had travelled all the way from the rural area to witness this moment. In the morning we took a photograph at New Neela studio along Tom Mboya Street then travelled lavishly dressed accompanied by other graduands to the Great Court, the field reserved for graduates to be. Daniel Arap Moi, who had taken over as the President of The Republic of Kenya in 1978 after the death of the first President, Jomo Kenyatta, presided over the Ceremony in his capacity as The Chancellor. It marked a great day for us since it was the closing of another chapter in our lives as well as the beginning of a new chapter.

We were on top of the world, seeing a great occasion we had waited for since our high school days come to pass. One could see each graduand in the presence of family members, some large enough to occupy two buses, songs and ululations everywhere. When the time for the award of degrees came, graduands were directed to their designated seats, grouped according to fields of achievement. As for us, Bachelor of Commerce Graduands, we were allocated seats in the front section, and each one of us would be later called to be awarded his or her Degree by the Vice Chancellor in the following manner

‘I give you the power to read and do all that appertains to this Degree’

Then came the partying. There were many parties that day. As for me I remember walking in the City Center majestically dressed in my academic gown and ending up at *Round about Estate* in the Company of My friend Ojowi. We had a nice party night. The rest is history.

Prior to our graduation, many potential employers had come to interview us for jobs. In those days jobs were readily available for all graduates. Majority of would be graduates were given appointment letters even before graduation, something which would become very uncommon in later years. As for me I had three letters of employment from which to choose; As a Supplies Officer 11 with The Ministry of Finance and Economic Planning, as a Trade Officer II with the ministry of Commerce and Industry and as an Officer with

Jackson Odeny Oyoo;   Memories of my life.

a Clearing and Forwarding Company in Mombasa. I chose to join The Ministry of Finance, and was seconded to Central Medical stores of The Ministry of Health.

Before posting to Central Medical Stores, we underwent an induction training within the parent ministry for a period of three weeks where we were trained on some guiding principles on Supplies Management including procurement, Stock control, Stores and Distribution management. At Central Medical Stores we had a further induction process by the Officer in Charge, Mr. Amos Kiriro. After the induction I was placed as The Stock Controller in charge of the paper entry process of medical stock up to the distribution process. To me this was quite challenging, but we steamed off the challenges by having lunch and two bottles of beer every working day at the nearby Landi Mawe bar. I wonder whether those facilities are still there.

I also remember a friend with whom we graduated from the same faculty, Mr. Oloo Omune who was posted at the nearby Ministry of Works Headquarters. We used to spend the greater part of the evening drinking beer. Our parting of ways came when he mistreated me on a visit to Uthiru where he used to stay. I never forgot how, when we had taken enough of the drink, he chased me out of his house in the middle of the night for no reason. We were overtaken with the drink. I had to take refuge in a nearby bar full of crooks. Anyway, those were very challenging times for a youth of my age.

It was also during this time that I was shown the door by my late uncle's wife at their residence in Landi Mawe, where I had taken refuge. But I cared the less since I was now an adult capable of taking care of myself.

Then life became more challenging when I moved to my own rental residence at Dandora phase 11. I now had to support myself in every way without relying on anybody. This is where I met my old friends at Miwani secondary School Mr. Silas Awiti who had secured a job with the Department of Registration of Persons and Mr. Jared Onyango Kokoro by then working with a company called TJ Cottington. I was paying a monthly rent of Shs. 400, no mean money those days. This is the house where I married my first wife Lovena Awuor, daughter of the late Mzee James Ong'ondo onjong'a and the late Mama Wlkister Otieno Onjong'a. I married Lovena through a traditional Marriage process in 1981 and Janet Nthambi, also through traditional marriage, in 1993.

Jackson Odeny Oyoo; Memories of my life.

By the way I am a polygamous man, married to two wives whom I love dearly in equal measure; lovena Awuor, whose parents are as mentioned and Janet Nthambi, daughter of Mzee Nelson Kalii Ndavi and Mama Ester Munyiva. Lovena has born me four children in the names of Anita Achieng (1982), Bruno Odhiambo (1985), Wilkister Otieno (1988), and Daisy Oyoo (1990). Janet has born me three children in the names of Francis Omondi (1994), Carolyne Atieno (1998) and Peter Onyango (2001). In total I have three sons and four daughters.

My first encounter with robbers was in mid1982, when I took leave from my place of work to travel home for a one month holiday. All things were prepared by my wife for the journey before we departed for the bus Station at around 800 PM. The plan was that Lovena would escort me, since I had a lot of luggage, to the bus stage and come back to the house after seeing me off. Little did we know that robbers would strike along the way, near Central Bus Park, throttle me by the neck and rob me of everything! My wife made a spirited resistance. As for me I just gave in and they run away with almost everything, including the watch I had just bought, presumably for display in the village. I was indeed

Jackson Odeny Oyoo;   Memories of my life.

disillusioned beyond measure. We had no choice but to cancel the journey and travel back to Dandora, our place of residence. The following day I went back to my place of work and cancelled the leave.

Dandora was a place of beehive activities especially during the night. I and my neighbor friends would go to work in the City center in the mornings and board our Matatus in the evenings for return journey, early enough to catch up with evening activities. We would then regroup, in the company of friends like Odhiambo, Arodi, Kokoro, Awiti, and others ready for the evening drink. We would drink even up to past midnight before retreat to our houses. When I reflect today, it was all but momentary happiness, living outside reality and lost. We would only think about the beer, not matters of personal development.

But I had one focus which lived my entire life; I made sure my younger brothers and sisters went to school. Wherever I went on transfers during my many tours of duty I carried them along the way. Indeed I paid school fees for my third born brother, the late Israel Ochieng with boom money. Boom money was money given in the form of student loans to support our various utilities while at the university. Much

Jackson Odeny Oyoo;   Memories of my life.

as I wasted this money on the drink, I never forgot to pay school fees for my siblings, thanks to that memorable cry of my father in his deathbed on 27th April 1963. I stood with them my entire university and working life.

Later on the ones who survived death would become academic giants in their own rights. Wilberforce Evans Omondi would go to a secondary school in Garissa where I was working in later years, then proceed to a University in India, and earn a bachelor of commerce Degree. He would rise through the ladders to become a Principal of a technical institution. Jenifer Nyamohanga would similarly go to a secondary school in Garissa, then together with her husband, start a private school in Nairobi which progressively became an academic giant. She would in the process also earn herself a university degree in the name of Bachelor of Early Childhood Development, an academic giant in her own right.

I am however sorry for my other brothers and sometimes wonder whether I provided the right leadership they required for their personal development. For my follower, Julius Kennedy Nyongo, he was an epitome of intellect, the brightest among us all. He earned a scholarship to learn in one of the best secondary schools of his time, Starehe Boys

Jackson Odeny Oyoo;   Memories of my life.

Center, and went on to pass his form four Exams with flying colors. He however lost direction along the way when he reached High School, having been admitted in the same school and after getting the requisite qualificationss. He took to drugs and this made him not go beyond High School as he had missed a paper during his form six exams. Although I later on managed to have him fixed in the same institution I was working, The Kenya Posts and Telecommunications Corporation, he never made it because of drugs. He was dismissed from service in 1996 and died a pauper in 2018. May the lord rest his soul in eternal peace.

Similarly my second follower Israel Ochieng, who also journeyed with me to every place I went, did not make it. Indeed I had played an extremely important part in his upbringing; having paid for his secondary school fees throughout from City High School using boom money, to Masii high School where he repeated third and fourth form. Having not done very well in his Form four examinations I managed to secure him a job as a clerical officer with The Kenya Posts in Carissa. I was doing everything for him to ensure that he had a stable life. He however took heavily to the drink which led to his premature demise in 2001.

Jackson Odeny Oyoo;   Memories of my life.

I'll be failing in my honesty if I don't remember my third born brother whom I also supported to ensure he had a good secondary education at Chulaimbo, finishing at Madogo Secondary school, Garissa with a good c+ pass. Dickens Otieno as he was named, was bright, hardworking and full of intellect. He however lost his life to drugs and died a mad person when the drug got a better part of his brain.

Therefore, much as I did in earnest to support my brothers and sisters, I had no control over their later year lives. I learnt a lesson never to play with the devil. If you do you will be crushed to pieces, however bright and intelligent you are. I will dwell on this in the concluding parts of this book.

My stint at The Central Medical Stores went on for one year. In December 1981, after applying for a job with the then Kenya Posts and Telecommunications Corporation, I was admitted as an Assistant Postal controller Trainee and called to join fellow trainees on 18th January 1982. At the training college we had some of the finest trainers in terms of discipline. There was this Trainer (they were called Instructors) Mr. Masila who brought sanity to our lives by instilling discipline in terms of time and attention to duty.

Jackson Odeny Oyoo;   Memories of my life.

We were trained on the basic principles of postal work, which included basic Postal account management, balancing of cash accounts and floor Supervision. This training did not go without hiccups, for at the time of our practical work, under the guidance of one Mr. Achiego, I incurred a shortage of KShs, 1,800, no mean money those days. This shortage almost caused me a mental breakdown, for I was required to make good immediately and I had not such an amount of money. Many things went through my head; could Mr. Achiego be the mastermind of this loss or was it sheer carelessness on my part. Anyway I put the case to rest and, let go my thoughts. I applied for a small loan to help in the recovery of the same.

Upon completion of the training, I was posted to The Postal Headquarters and placed to work in the mails department as an Assistant Postal Controller Domestic Mails. Here I worked under a Mr. Ombewa who was the Principal controller. An astute, tall man with great practical knowledge on domestic mail network. Mr. Ombewa gave me the first praccal knowledge of mail network and travelled with me to the farthest parts of our country introducing me to live mail network. I wonder whether he is still alive.

Jackson Odeny Oyoo;   Memories of my life.

I had a short stint of one year working in Domestic Mails before I was transferred to Machakos in 1994, to be an Assistant Postal Controller under Mr. Kieti who was the Postal Manager. Mr. Kieti happens to be one of the kindest people I worked under. He travelled with me places in the line of Inspection and Audit work. I got the opportunity to know Machakos region, then known as Eastern Division in Psotal segregation terms. I travelled to places like Matuu, Kitui, Makueni, Mitaboni, Athi River, Masii, Mtito Andei, indeed all stations in Eastern Division. Wherever we went Mr. Kieti would introduce us to goat meat (nyama choma) and beers which would go even past midnight. I do not know whether this was happiness, but on the whole I enjoyed my stay at Machakos. This is the place where our second born child Bruno Odhiambo was born. He has now grown his age and works in Doha, Qattar.

Again after a short stint at Machakos I was transferred to Garissa to head the Postal Department of the newly created Eastern Diviion from the Larger Eastern Division which was renamed Southern Division. This posting was all excitement as I had my opportunity to be a manager in a corporation as large as the then Kenya Posts and Telecommunications

Corporation. I was on my own, only reporting to one boss, not a line of bosses. In other words I was the second top most person in the region, made critical decisions affecting postal operations including travelling any place I desired in the course of duty. Garissa was a Provincial Headquaters of the Kenya Government, this meant I brushed shoulders with top most people in the province, from the Provincial Commissioner to Provincial Departmental Heads. I remember a Mr. Ogolla who was the Provincial Director of Social Services, who became a very dear friend and with whom we travelled all social places, drinking beers and attending parties.

Sometimes I would travel more than 60 kilometers away to Bura Tana, then Hola, both in Tana River District in line of duty. We usually went to these stations to do inspection of Accounts and other audit work. In the evenings we would team up with the local staff and merry, just as we used to do in Machakos and Garissa.

This was the pattern of my life in Southern and Eastern Divisions of The Kenya Posts. Only one thing stood out in a very positive way; I neither forgot my brothers nor my sisters nor my mother. Wherever I was posted I was with them. In

Machakos I was with Israel my second follower; In Garissa I was with Israel, Wilberforce and Jenifer, making sure that they went through with their secondary school to the end.

The memory of my Father's cry that evening of 27th April 1963 never left me, the cry of a dying father desperately searching the winds on who would rescue his children after his death. My uncle Hezbon kept on reminding me why they took me to school, and for sure, I never disappointed them. I keep on parting myself for this earthly wisdom which came from my father, may his soul continue resting in peace as his will was fulfilled.

My mother visited me every month in Machakos. I now reflect it was the love of a mother yearning for a son she dearly loved. She was however, hypertensive, and visited in search of medicine to control the blood pressure. In those days such medicines were rare and costly. Her ignorant mind, I believe, could not come to terms that such medicines were also available in our local majot Town of Kisumu. So she travelled all the way yearning to see me and to look for her medicine. For sure, I never disappointed her. As I moved to Garissa, the long distance could not allow her to travel every month. She nevertheless, visited us occasionally between every three to six months. For sure I always ensured she had enough stock of medicine to last her for a minimum of three months.

Even though my mother would stay home for the next minimum three months, I ensured we had a talk every Monday. In those days making a phone call was one of the most difficult, if not expensive things to do. There were no direct calls, hence mother would travel to Kisumu and be connected to me using the facilitation of Telecommunications staff in Kisumu. After talking with her I would arrange to send her money using Telegraph Money order service, and this would also be facilitated by Kisumu Postal staff. The whole idea was to keep her going on without any stress and in this way I was indeed able to ensure stability of her blood pressure. She would wait for at least five hours around Kisumu offices before the finalization of the money order processing into cash. A normal money order transmission would take at least two days to process. When we reflect back from the present M-pesa system, it is only delighting to appreciate that we have come from far. The current system is within seconds, yet the old one took two days in the least.

Jackson Odeny Oyoo;   Memories of my life.

My quest for the education for my brothers was a great struggle in search of resources. I think I did not balance my finances very well because the better part went on alcohol. But I struggled to ensure they had the best education. Indeed when my young brother Wilberforce passed his exams with good grades, I ensured he went for a degree in India. India was the second alternative for those who did not secure chances in the two local Universities. So through fundraising together with my friends we took my brother to India. I was aware he went through serious challenges in India, the challenges of meeting course fees and subsistence allowance. Nevertheless, being the enduring person he was, he finished his education and came back with a university degree. That was a great pat on his back.

My first taste of God was in Garissa. One of the friends of my youthful years Mr. Jared Oloo Ombwa had already received Jesus Christ as his savior and he made sure he brought me the word of God all the way from home, in the Company of his Pastor Patroba Ojwang and another fellow Pastor from Ahero church. This touched me and somehow I started entering slowly into this strange kingdom called God's Kingdom. It was strange to me because sideways some other sect of religionists used to visit us in Garissa undertaking cleansing activities with some 'signs and wonders', not in the name of Jesus but in the name of their god Messiah Ondeto. This one was called Legio Maria, talking religious issues with no Holy Bible backups. I have come to the rude realization that I should never have involved myself with this sect in the first place. In the second art of this book I have gone into great detail about the God whom I serve now, with all my heart and strength.

My tour of duty in Garissa lasted seven years before I was posted back to Nairobi in 1992, upon my promotion to the rank of Senior Postal Controller. At Nairobi I was assigned to handle international mails, a job I handled with a lot of passion and zeal. Sometimes I would also travel with the top most man in the Planning and Development line, Mr. Gerald Oruccoson, then Chief Postal Controller, who became my best friend even though he was in a very top seat. We would travel with him places in the line of duty. My first international assignment to undertake some research work on International Mail Accounting in Dare Salam, Tanzania was initiated by him.

We went to Tanzania with a colleague who was a chief Trainer in mails at The Kenya College of Communications and Technology a Mr. Fred Kavinguha. This was my first good taste of the good things of the worldly life. For this assignment I was paid $4.000 for the whole journey, which worked out to Kenya Shs, 280.000. I ended up in Dar with almost $3,000 in my pocket with no plans at all on how to spend it. I had only spent $1,000 in Nairobi and travelled with the balance to Tanzania. We had what life would give us in the moment, the beers, the women, the night dances. Looking back, it was a terrible life which I now regret.

Nevertheless, this was the place where I was introduced to International Accounts and which would later on open doors of opportunity for me at the Post Office. It did not take long before I was promoted to An Assistant Manager in charge of International Mails Accounts. This is the place where I made the most impact in my work at the Post Office. I was the officer in charge, in control of everything international mails, in fact even in the operational aspects.

I realized the authoritative knowledge on international mail discipline was lacking, both in operational and Accounting aspects. I was given the opportunity to revolutionize, the way of thinking and behaving when it became aspects to do international mails. I came to the knowledge that despite receiving quite a voluminous mails from countries abroad, billings had not been done in equal measure. In the end, the Kenya Posts and Telecommunications Corporation ended up losing a lot of money, in terms tens of thousands of dollars. I also came to uncover rackets done by international mails conmen, most of them non Kenyan citizens living abroad. They were done in such a way that only international mail experts would be able to uncover, something which I did with the background knowledge I received from my training, thanks to the Head of Postal services during this time, Mr. Charles Muga who supported me fully and gave me the will to undertake this work from all angles.

My greatest undoing was when I requested for a transfer to work in Kisumu, my home City. It was accepted, and I was posted to work as the assistant to the Regional manager. It was from this time that I made the most blunders in my working life. This was in 1996. The blunders ranged from the indiscipline I exercised in my work place to the social aspects of my life.

First, I entered into wrong companies. My boss was an alcoholic and I followed in this line without blinking. I gradually became an alcoholic, not caring about the times of reporting to work, equally following the footsteps of my boss. I would be working in Kisumu every day from my home village. I owe a great gratitude to the lord, because, despite driving all the way from home village every day to Kisumu, 40 kilometers away, I never had an accident. I am equally convinced that the lord was preparing me for t5he work ahead. That's why my life was preserved, nothing more. I was no better than the alcoholics I used to meet every day on the road, causing serious accidents. In the end the work I was doing my work very irresponsibly and the overall work suffered. The Tone at the top was lacking from both of us.

Secondly my family life became a disarray. I found myself reaching home every day past midnight because of long bar brawls. Also on equal measure, I made my driver become an alcoholic, because he would be in my company most of these times and he had no control over my misbehavior. We would be engaging ourselves in drinking the nights away with unknown people, some of them women with dubious backgrounds. I can now face myself bravely and say I had a

Jackson Odeny Oyoo;   Memories of my life.

loose uncontrolled life which injured the closest people to me.

This kind of life went on for some time before I was shown the door. Our seniors at the Headquarters became uneasy with our performance. So we ended up (me and my boss) being interdicted and eventually forcefully retired from the service of the Kenya Posts.

On the other hand my forceful retirement from work was a blessing in disguise. It was immediately after retirement that I began searching my soul. I came to the rude realization that I had been lost and now I was found by other forces beyond my control; the forces of rejection, of withdrawal and of self-examination. Somehow I found the answers, too little too late. I was now in my own company of rejection, trying not to be with familiar faces and always retiring into a cocoon of my own.

But the worst came with the symptoms of forceful retirement: withdrawal, hunger, anger, being beaten to eat the humble pie, self-denial, cruelty and all the negative dispositions. I also found it very difficult to sleep at night. The nightmares I used to experience at my years in the University

Jackson Odeny Oyoo;   Memories of my life.

came back with a bang. I would be frequently attacked by bad dreams; people chasing me at night to kill me, and at times dreams about being in the company of my alcoholic friends. I had already withdrawn from alcohol, but these old friends would come to me in dreams forcing me to take alcohol against my will. I was fighting all the times at night with very powerful bodiless forces.

Jackson Odeny Oyoo;   Memories of my life.

CHAPTER 6

THE SECOND WILDERNESS EXPERIENCE: Sustained by the grace of God.

Whereas the first wilderness experience was concerning getting direction after the loss of my father, the second wilderness experience concerned getting direction after the loss of my first formal employment. Both experiences had a great impact on my life, for they would seal my understanding of the value of life. They would help me to fill the void in my life which neither education nor having a good job with good income would not do.

It was the grace of God that sustained me after my retirement from Kenya Posts in1999, and for the next 14 years. I decided to quit alcohol, having recognized the great damage it had done to my life. I made an irrevocable decision to serve God. This is a matter I will deal with in the later chapters,

My first wife, even though still having her job also at Kenya Posts and Telecommunications Corporation, had to come to terms with the reality that she was the sole bread winner for her children. Here was a young woman in Nairobi City, having

Jackson Odeny Oyoo;   Memories of my life.

to shoulder the burden of paying for the children to go to school, in terms of their transport every day to and from school and their school fees. This was particularly so for the last two who were still in Primary School. The first two were already in Secondary school. It was indeed my responsibility to ensure that they finished their secondary education. God was on my side, for even though they were sent home now and then because of non-payment of fees, they managed to go through. Indeed they passed well enough to proceed with further education.

At home was my second wife, with no livelihood support since she had not been in any employment, formal or informal. Here we also were, with two children aged 2 years and 5 years requiring the most basic necessities of life which were not available. The priorities here included food and clothing which were extremely difficult to afford. As for shelter, I had put up some two temporary structures, one for my first wife and the other for the second one. Even though they were somehow dilapidated, they did not fall in the list of my priorities for implementation.

 I will always thank the Lord my God, for even though we had no steady income, we were always assured of our daily bread. We never slept hungry all those dry years between 1999 and 2009, for somehow along the way I had small contracts for my sustenance. One thing I made sure not to do was to go back to my old habits. I always mourned over the pain I had caused everybody including me because of my past alcoholism state. I thought, and I was very right, that I would rather go hungry than coil another crooked means of earning a living which in the long run would cause me worse pain.

So I got myself different jobs to support our livelihood. The first one which came my way was a teaching job at a small polytechnic Institute in Chemelil, where I was placed to head the Institution. Our income as teachers at the institute depended entirely on the number of students we recruited, a tall order in the area. Nevertheless we struggled and ensured we had the barest necessities good enough to share with the family at home. I stayed here for six months while trying to locate my bearing for the next move. The second and subsequent jobs involved getting Government contracts' ranging from desilting of rivers in my home area to renovating Government houses in the region. These ones were better because one contract alone would sustain me for a reasonable period before I got the next one.

Jackson Odeny Oyoo;   Memories of my life.

Despite all these challenges, what was imprinted on my heart by my dying father more than five decades back never left my memory and became indelible all the way. Somehow I ensured that all my children went to the best affordable schools, the ones at the village attended private schools three kilometers away at Katito. The older ones from my first wife were now grown and ended up in good secondary schools in my province, then called Nyanza province. As I continued trusting on God new opportunities lingered in bits and pieces, which not only sustained me, but drove me deeper into trusting God.

I also had an opportunity to endear myself with the elders of my home area. I interacted with some, I would say, likeminded colleagues although in the older age bracket. These included retired educationists Christopher Ojienda, Augustine Mumma, the late John Odingo, the late John Rasare and Professor Kapiyo, men who opened up for me and mentored me to the social aspects of life. Together we started Nyakach Elders Development Group, a vehicle which was used to bring the elders of Nyakach district, now called Nyakach Sub County together. We also initiated a non-governmental program to address health and other social concerns in the District, such as abject poverty, HIV menace, flood mitigation and the like. The program was of great benefit to the region, to the extent that we registered an NGO (Non-governmental Organization) called Sondu Miriu Nam Awach Development Organization (SOMNADO) to enable liaison with Government and other agencies, local and international.

In 2009, I had my first breakthrough when I was called upon to undertake a human resource management job at Sondu Miriu Electricity Project. This was better because I now had regular monthly income which enabled me to pay school fees with ease. My stint at Sondu Miriu lasted a few years before I landed the major breakthrough which opened doors to greater opportunities.

This was when I was appointed by the County Government of Kisumu to serve as a Commissioner with the County Public Service Board. Here I was earning quite a reasonable salary which enabled me to construct two permanent houses for my two wives in different homes. I sustained my recovery to self-awareness, even the awareness of the great potential which existed within me. I was able to travel places both within and outside the country. During the five years that I

Jackson Odeny Oyoo;   Memories of my life.

served in the Board I travelled such places as Mombasa, Eldoret, Nakuru, Kakamega, Siaya, Nairobi and Naivasha in line of the duty I had been assigned to do: serving as the Committee chairman of Human Resource Audit and Performance Management. I equally travelled to Tanzania, South Africa and Israel in line of further Training.

In Israel I visited most of the Biblical sites like the site where Jesus was baptized in River Jordan; the Sea of Galilee; Jerusalem sites of Gethsemane, the Great old wall, and the parliament of Israel. We even saw the site where Jesus was crucified and buried before he resurrected.

Such was my life in the wilderness after I had been shown the door from Kenya Posts: a life which was full of mountains and valleys, but which nevertheless was sustained not by my own power but by the grace of God.

CHAPTER 7

MY HUMAN ROOTS: GENEALOGY TO PRESENT DAY COMMUNITY OF GEM RAE PEOPLE

As I have said before, the scanty information I received from the older people of my preceding generation and from men and women of historical knowledge were synchronized to become integral information upon which I built the story of my ancestral roots. Though scanty, the information made me to establish some pattern about the roots. In the end I came up with what I call my own summary, for which I am proud and take full responsibility.

Having come to the conclusion that my tap root ancestor was **Luo Ganda**, I now proceed from my immediate ancestors in the land of my inheritance. It is worth noting that the present day Gem Rae is inhabited by people who were generated from three distantly interrelated clans, Nyangla Oremo, Kawakungu and Kanyikwaya. I will restrict my story to the ancestor of my origins, Nyangla Oremo.

NYANGLA OREMO was my 6th great grandfather to whom I owe my direct ancestry. The generation of Nyangla Oremo inhabit the major part of the present day Gem Rae. He had

Jackson Odeny Oyoo;   Memories of my life.

three wives, which form the present day community of Gem Rae people. They were:

1. Wamoya from Alego Kaugagi who begot two sons **Bele** and **Rabok**
2. Apindi from Maragoli who begot Oloo Sirembe
3. Abuor from Kokidi who begot **Oloo Ranyach, Okech Rach and Osano Ajwang**

The above wives of Nyangla Oremo make the major clans of Gem Rae known as the five sub clans of: JOKA BELE, JOKARABOK, JOKA OLOO RANYACH, JOKA OKECH RACH AND JOKA OSANO AJWANG. In a simplified manner I was able to cluster them in the following ways:

I.BELE had two wives Arach from Alego and Nyanjawa also from Alego.

Arach begot Oyugi (present families of Johana Okunga, Ondoi Owuondo, Aloyce Andoga, Okello Nyang', Okwanyo Mikola, Ombwa Mikola and others.

Nyanjawa begot Adel and Sirero

II.RABOK had four wives;

Jackson Odeny Oyoo;   Memories of my life.

- Onjaro from Alego from where the families of opiyo Ogwadu and Kamire sprang.
- Nyachia from Alego Kogelo from which sprang the families of Ogero, Oywoya (the father of Oyosi), Okech, Owuor, Opudo, Owich Kamakiri and others
- Didi from Alego from which sprang the families of Dol (who migrated to kobongo in Kano) and Amadi (the father of Ombara and his kinsmen)
- Achach from Alego who begot Nyagol from which sprang the families of Oledho, Agwaya Ochikre, Nyapande Ogonda, Nyagol Soro and others

III.OLOO SIREMBE had no known descedants.

IV.OLOO RANYACH had three wives; Atieno from Maragoli, Bege from Jimo and Arodi from Katolo who bore the following

- From Atieno sprang the families of Ogada (the father of Dishon Okelo and others), Nyanungo (the father of Dishon Kwach and others) Ojuok (the father of Narkiso Omuom and others), Akach (the father of Joel Okelo and others) and others

Jackson Odeny Oyoo; Memories of my life.

o From Bege sprang the families of Katho (the father of Awino whose daughter Ojalo was given to Andang'o in return for a ritual of traditional importance), Aguyo, Noah Oloo and Obong'o Dida.

o From Arodi sprang the following families ; Nyandere, Omware, Ishmael Oyare, Ater, Okombo, Adidi the story teller and others

V.OKECH RACH had two sons, OLEWE and NYAKWAMBA

o From Olewe sprang the following families: Ongele: Ogwambo, Ater who died a bachelor and Abongo who migrated to South Nyanza.

o From Nyakwamba sprang the following families: Magak, Odongo, Ogal, Ongor, Udo, Olewe, Gone and Magak, Killeon Oburu, Mwatha, Mijude, Otieno, Dan, Jayalo and others.

VI. My grear great grandfather **OSANO AJWANG** had four wives; Diang'a from Alego Usonga, Jieyi from Kabuoch, Nyadiem from Kokidi and De from Kabuoch. His descedants are the following;

1.   **DIANG'A the first wife of Osano** had three sons from which sprang the following families;

i.Dianga's first son Ogelo Orayo, Offspring:

Bute Nyarem, Osano Ogonyo, Katho, Lango Ongudi, Walter Osimbo, Tom Osimbo, Assistant Chief Aomo, Reuben Osimbo and others,

ii.Dianga's Second son Otieno Nyakaka ofspring:

Otieno Nyakaka's first son Nyamango, Offspring:
Osano Aluko, Ogello, Otieno, Mbom, and Nyamango, Awino, Oloo, Aluko, Owili, Odanga, Owuoca and Joel Otieno, Adela, Omwandu, Mathayo Amonde, Jacob Ayodo, Okwanyo, Jeremiah Ngwena, Francis Abongo, Jacob Juma, Zedekiah Osano, Orayo, Aluko, Akeyo, Timbo, Tobias Adoyo, Thoma (Benson Otieno), Zacharia Ouma, Elisha Omondi, Ibrahim Kayo, Robert Otieno

Jackson Odeny Oyoo;   Memories of my life.

Otieno Nyakaka's second son Luth, offspring:

Omolo Raywende, Nyamango, Ogelo and Asewe. Ogwang' ,Ongaro, Ongor, Siem, Obumba, Amonde, Amonde, Obudho, Muga, Awino, Gerphas Omolo, Obumba, Amonde, Adoyo, Owili Oteng'o, Adidi, Ongor, Obudho, Owili, Owuocha, Ambrose Abongo, Anton Obango, Muga, John Odada, Paul Omundo, Rawo, Odenya, Yoo, Muga, Manya, Akach, Nyongo, Rapudo, Obango, Mudho, Adongo, Odhiambo, Owili Otengo, Nyakiti, Opepo, sasi, Nobert Odhiambo and others.

iii.Dianga's third son Mudho offspring:

Mudho had seven wives: Nyakongo from nyakongo South Nyanza; Asik Nyoyier from Kakwa Juok; Owuocha from Nyakongo; Ogonda from Kakwa Juok; Abong'a from Kanyaluo and Amolo from Kanyakwar.

They form the present day generation of JOKAMUDHO, segregated as follows;

Nyakongo offspring: Families of Ogelo, Wadanda(Ongor, Obiny and Ongenge), Ondiek (Abungu, Ochele, Akowa,

Agonga and Wajango), Adie (Owuocha, Lange, Ajwang and Okello) Wende   (Danga, Olala And Onyiego) and Others

Asik offspring : Families of Ajode, Akuku, Omore, Ong'or, Wendo, samwel Oyare, Otieno, Aiko, joram Omoth, Peter Owuocha, Christopher Osimbo, Hezekia Achia, Ndago Omoth, Oudu , joka Otieno, Osimbo Bonyo, Owee, Ong'or, Bonyo, Otieno, ogaya Munda, Ajode, Adie, Apunda, Nyafwamba, Okech, Ong'or, Owuocha, Otieno Chogo, Oyare, Bonyo, Otieno, Zephania Odayo, Japheth Awino, Gilbert Owuocha, Michael Aduda, Samson Apum, Elekia Ong'or, Claudias Oyare, James Obwa, John Asewe and others.

Owuocha offspring; Mudho, Adede, Oyare, Ogweno, Okwanyo, Nyong'o, Gilbert Ogolla, Charles Odera, Robert Ayoo, Boaz Otieno, Ongor, Hosea Lusi and others.

Abonga offspring: Tina Aoro, Mudho Oneno, Nyamanga, Ajode, Aroko, Orwaga and others.

Ogonda offspring; Bute, Akello, Sila Osambo, Agwambo and others.

Jackson Odeny Oyoo; Memories of my life.

Amollo offspring; Ndia, Muga and others.

2. My grear great grandmother **JIEYI,** the second wife of Osano had two sons, **Oyoo and Ndia:**

The first born son of Jieyi , Oyoo, is the sub clan from which I owe my direct generation. His tree spreads as follows;

Oyoo had three wives which form three main offspring of the present day   **JOKOYOO SUB CLAN**: 1. OLOO MARIENGA from Koguta 2. AWILI from Koguta and 3. ABONGO NYAR KOKO.

- OLOO MARIENGA had one son OLOO who begot Zakayo Jabuya and Nyong'o. Jabuya married Leya nyar Wamunga from Luanda, (the region of the rain makers as was then known) and had the following three sons; Daniel Akowa, Edward Oyoo and Nashon Owuocha. Oloo Marienga's other son NYONG'O married Regina Oloo nyar Umala from Gem Kathomo and had two sons Amos Ochong and Henry Amimo.

- o AWILI begot one son called JIEYI (named after Oyoo's mother) who begot Nyong'o who begot three sons Otimo, Otulo and Oyugi.

- o ABONG'O NYAR KOKO had four sons; 1. Omolo the husband of Ludia Adoyo who died at a fairly young age, 2. Ombayi (the father of Jonam Akowa), 3. Danga (the father of Christopher Omolo and Hanningtone Gone) and 4. Nyamulo who died fatherless. Ludia took care of Jonam Akowa, Christopher Omolo and Hannington Gone, since their mother Abong'o nyar Koko died when they were very young. She died at a prime old of over 80 years in the 1970's.

Since Zakayo Jabuya was my grandfather, I wish to revisit his tree in greaterdetail as follows: The first born son of Zakayo Jabuya, Daniel Akowa, married Zilpa Omore Nyasawo from Kagwel sub clan of Kabodho with whom they had eight children; Abigael Odongo who was married to Samuel Nyanganga Ogilo in Uyoma, Penina Anyango who was married in the Kobala clan of South Nyanza, Atieno who was the co-wife of his sister Abigael Odongo to Samuel

Jackson Odeny Oyoo;   Memories of my life.

Nyanganga, Caleb Auma who married Pamela nyar Kobala, Achieng who was married in Uyoma to Nyanganga's brother Otumba Ogilo, Dr. Akowa, Lea who was married to George Obongo of Kobala, and Millicent Akinyi who was married in Kobala. The immediate children of Daniel Akowa are dead except for Millicent Akinyi who now lives in Kobala as a widow, having lost her husband at a young age.

The second born son of Jabuya, Edward Oyoo married Jane Anyango Nyamajanga, from Kabar kogolla, with whom he had nine children; Alice Akinyi who became married to Washinton Ouma Aseda of Oyugis South nyanza; Jackson Odeny (the author) who became married to lovena Awuor daughter of James Onjonga of Kotieno, South Nyanza and Janet Nthambi daughter of Nelson Ndavi Kalii of Lita, Machakos; Abraham who died when still a baby; Julius Nyongo who married Zilpa of Kokwanyo village in South Nyanza; Israel Ochieng who married Grace Atieno of Kendu Bay, Emily Atieno of Busia and Mary Adhiambo of Koguta, Nyakach; Evans Wilberforce Omondi who married Beatrice Anyango of Kadem, South Nyanza; Dickens Otieno who died a bachelor; Jenifer Aluoch who married Julius Nyamohanga of Kuria tribe and Nerea Omolo who got married in South Nyanza.

The third born son of Zakayo Jabuya, Nashon Owuocha, had three wives Sarah Nyar Abiero from Kabonyo with whom he bore five daughters (Atieno, Awuor, Jackline , Betha and Night), Alice nyar Ombija from Kabondo with whom he bore three sons (Elvis Odiwuor, Okura, Francis Obara) and one daughter Faith Achieng and Zilpa nyar Ombija from Kabondo with whom he bore two sons (Elisha Ollando and Levis Okoth), and two daughters; Hellen Achieng and Mercy Awuor . Alice and Zilpa were sisters, both daughters of Ombija.

The second born son of Jieyi was **Ndia.** His tree has spread as follows;

The following offspring sprang from Ndia

- o   Ndia's   wife, Okelo Nyagong, offspring; the families of Iro, Okoko, Nyandere, Otimo and others,

- o   Ndia's wife Auma, offspring; the families of Were Odumo, Afwata, Obwa and others

Jackson Odeny Oyoo;   Memories of my life.

o   Ndia's wife Widu, offspring; the families of Owaka Ninga, Arach, Adie, Okongo and others.

NB How the wives follow one another is not known

3.   NYADIEM, the third wife of Osano:

Migrated to Ringa Kakelo from which there are the families of Obumba lak Rang'iela the father of Omollo

4.   DEE, the fourth wife of Osano;

This is where the families of **Ayoo** the father of Francis Mudho and Olang sprang from; Dee was placed under Jieyi by virtue of coming from the same home of Kabuoch (referred to as *nyar od Jieyi*). She was a close relative of Jieyi.

My grandfather Zakayo Jabuya contributed immensely to the development of education in Gem Rae. He championed for the introduction of formal education by carrying the blackboard all the way from Maseno and through making sure, together with his likeminded friend, Elisha Ollando that all school age children went to school. This was no mean achievement, for a blackboard used in teaching was indeed a very rare commodity. Carrying it all the way from Maseno, 60 kilometers away was indeed a great struggle, considering that there was no motor transport. People used to travel to and from Maseno on foot.

I was told this blackboard was not an empty blackboard. On it were already inscribed written messages of mathematics and English which would be taught to Gem Rae pupils for a time. When the messages taught were exhausted Zakayo would go back to Maseno for new Messages and carry them the same way to Gem Rae. This was the kind of zeal my grandfather had for education.

My grandfather's efforts gradually paid off at his family level, for in the end he succeeded in giving good education to his own son Edward Oyoo who was my father. Edward went through Primary school with success and ended up as a trained teacher, having undertaken his training at Maseno College. I was told that he taught English and mathematics with great zeal and that at the time of his premature death in 1963, he was considered as one of the best brains within the teaching fraternity.

I would be failing in my honesty if I don't recall the fact that Gem Rae village, small as it is,   was an epitome of zeal in

Jackson Odeny Oyoo;   Memories of my life.

education and religion. This zeal made it to produce some of the greatest minds that this Country has ever had.

In the field of academics there were great Scholars like Professor Okoth Ogendo, the University Guru of Land Law; Professor Agabo Ochong the great Scholar of Maseno University; Professor of Medicine Gideon Okello; Engineer Dr. Pius Okello Odiko and his wife Mary Okello, the Founders of Makini Schools, one the greatest academic institutions this country has ever had; Mr. Okech Oguma, a land surveyor of repute; Ochola Ogoda, a quantity surveyor also of repute; Professor Tom ojienda, a lawyer, scholar who served up to the highest level of Law governance in this Country; his father Christopher Ojienda, A historian and a great educationist in Kenya; Engineer Maurice Chore a Civil Engineer serving with the Government of Kenya.

I will always mention the name of my grandfather Zakayo Jabuya as the one who ignited the education zeal in Gem Rae.

In the field of Religion, the first church in Gem Rae, The African inland Mission (AIM), arrived in the first decade of the twentieth Century. It was locally led by Luka Aluko, followed by the Anglican Church led by my grandfather Zakayo Jabuya.

Jackson Odeny Oyoo;   Memories of my life.

The last one to arrive was The Catholic church led by Girpus Omolo. The person who taught the word of God in the Anglican Church with zeal was however Elisha Ollando, and his work was translated into the development of staunch men of faith like Obaje Iro, Allan Iro, Ong'or Iro, Oyare Otieno, Odingo Owe and others.

Along with these educational and religious developments were also men of means. Riches were reflected in the amount of livestock one possessed. The men who fitted this cadre included Oyosi wuon Oyuoya, Orina, Osano Oguya, Ong'or Obiny, Otieno wuon Ogonda and Angong'a Janjore. They had innumerable number of cattle, sheep and goats.

Jackson Odeny Oyoo; Memories of my life.

PART TWO

My Life

In

God's Kingdom

CHAPTER 8

THE TRANSITION FROM WORLDLY VALUES AND TO KINGDOM VALUES

1. Introduction

As mentioned in my preface I discovered that my ancestral roots limit me as to my total being or my whole heritage. As a matter of fact the roots only helped me to identify the idiosyncrasies in my life and to know that I am a subject of limitations if I refuse to recognize that I owe my total being to a higher power without limits. I fully acknowledged the identity of my whole self with the divine nature of my lord and savior, Jesus Christ. I accepted his mentorship, having escaped the putridity of the world brought about by my carnal heritage.

In part one of this book I have demonstrated in great detail what it means when a Christian talks about 'walking in the flesh'. I am not ashamed to say that I spent the better part of my life gratifying the desires of my flesh, from my primary school days through secondary school up to the university and beyond. Even though we spent some of our times, particularly Sundays, in church, I did not know God. I neither

Jackson Odeny Oyoo;   Memories of my life.

drew nearer to him nor talked about him. In other words my heart was very far from him.

In my secondary school days, as I approached my form four exams, I became very sick, to the point that my mother was helpless. There was a time that I could not sleep at night, suffering from hallucinations. Whenever I tried to sleep, some evil spirits would haunt me and instill great fear in me. Because of this great fear my paternal uncle, Nashon Owuocha, would take me to sleep beside him in his home, in the hope that I would gain enough courage to overcome the fears. It did not work.

It reached a time that a traditional doctor, I remember his name as Aoko Jakri, was invited to spell the bad omens. In the process a sacrifice of a lamb was made, to spill out blood, onstetively to please the evil spirits. It did not work. They just cooled them enough to allow me go back to school in order to finish my education.

At the university I was determined to pursue my education to the finish line. Despite these bad spells, I had made a covenant with my heart that I must continue with education whatever the circumstances. So I struggled, fearing to sleep at night with the lights off. My roommate, I remember him as Okemwa, always wondered why I had the lights on, contrary to what happened in the other rooms. I was driven by great fear which I never explained to anybody. I thought I owed nobody any reason for my behavior.

I spent most of my free times in wrong company, always desiring to travel places for the purpose of drinking alcohol and sleeping with women whose background I cared little to know about. This culture of life continued up to my years in formal employment. I was now married to two women, but some erratic force drove me from them. I made them helpless. Deep inside me I cried for help which never came. My life was empty full of hatreds and the unforgivenesses of my youth. Who would save me from this wretchedness of life, I kept asking myself.

There reached a time that I would no longer hold to my job as I kept on being the drunkard I was even during working times. This misbehavior led to my forced retirement in 1998. With my retirement was the beginning of another life of frustration, having mouths to feed with no means at all. The money was gone and all my earthly friends departed from me. I was left alone travelling the fast road to my grave.

Jackson Odeny Oyoo; Memories of my life.

### 2.	The realization, coming to terms with self

It was during this very difficult season of my life that I realized that I needed help. My friends had deserted me and I now found myself in the middle of the 'never do wells in the village'. Of course abuses and insults were occasionally hurled at me such as

So you can now be found within us, why your education can't help you!!...
If you cannot afford beer why don't you join us in the local brew, chang'aa club!!...
Do not talk in front of us. You have nothing to show us....

We have seen many people come and go.
We are not surprised that you are also on the way!!......

These were very bitter words to somebody who had been placed in the higher echelons of society. I had already migrated from both Nairobi and Kisumu cities and was now a permanent resident of my rural Gem Rae village.

Jackson Odeny Oyoo;   Memories of my life.

The realization that nobody, not even any magician would rescue me, from the dungeon of the sins I had committed against myself, against the people close to me and the organizations I had worked for (my wives, my children, my relatives, my friends and my former employers) deeply affected me. I became overly convinced that there was only one savior who could come to my rescue, the lord Jesus Christ. But one question lingered on my mind, how was Jesus Christ going to rescue me? This was a matter I had to deal with whatever the circumstances.

3. Convicted of sin

I became convicted of sin and further realized that the lord must come into my life. I cannot remember what happened, but I suddenly found myself mourning over my sins and calling loud on the name of Jesus Christ in my Gem Rae house, saying

Lord Jesus come to my rescue……….
I have sinned against many people and against you……….
Deliver me from the slavery of sin…………..
I am helpless……….

Jackson Odeny Oyoo;   Memories of my life.

For sure I became fully convinced that the spirit of the Lord had come into my life. The Bible suddenly became live and a very precious book to me. I started reading the Bible. Every word of the lord gave meaning to my life. What I really wanted to know was not only Jesus but also to experience his power in my life. Some of his words were quickly internalized in my heart:

'The time is fulfilled and the Kingdom of God is at hand. Repent and believe the gospel. **Mark 1; 15**

Come to me, all you who are weary and burdened, and I will give you rest. Take my yoke upon you and learn from me, for I am gentle and humble in heart, and you will find rest for your souls. **Mathews 11; 28 – 29**

I was also concerned about my polygamous position as I found myself with two wives with whom I had seven children in total. How would I handle this?

I was convinced that even in the Old Testament Patriarchs like Abraham and David were polygamous. This did not prevent them from being men after God's heart and they are

Jackson Odeny Oyoo;   Memories of my life.

now in heaven. Abraham had at least Sarah, Hagar and Keturah as his wives and David had at least Michal and Bathsheba. They walked lives of faith.

Indeed the lord says of David in **1 Samuel 16; 7**

'The lord does not look at things people look at. People look at the outward appearance, but the lord looks at the heart'

And in 2 Samuel 7; 16, the Lord says

'Your house and you kingdom will endure forever before me. Your throne will be established forever'

Elsewhere, concerning change of status in a family from darkness to light, where one partner becomes a believer and the other is not, Paul says **in 1 Corinthians 7; (NIV),**

Verse 15: But if the unbelieving depart, let him depart. A brother or a sister is not under bondage in such cases. But God has called us to peace.

Verse 16: How do you know wife, whether you will save your husband? Or how do you know, husband, whether you will save your wife?

Jackson Odeny Oyoo; Memories of my life.

Verse 24: *Brothers and sisters, each person, as responsible to God, should remain in the same situation they were in when God called them.*

For me to put these internal conflicts to rest, I decided to stick with my wives and children, for the sake of my peace and their peace. I already had four children with my first wife and three children with the second wife. They had nowhere to go. They did not leave me and I also did not leave them.

I decided once and for all to give my life to Jesus, to surrender my soul to the Lord and to be serious with going to the church. I confessed my sins in church and asked the lord for forgiveness.

I became a member of The Voice and Salvation Church for a while, moved to Chrisco Church before landing in the Ministry of Repentance and Holiness. I am convinced the message of the lord is one and the same. Churches are buildings and institutions for convenience in fellowshipping and worshipping the lord together. They cannot replace our bodies which are transformed to become temples of the Holy

Jackson Odeny Oyoo;   Memories of my life.

Spirit **(1 Corinthians 6:19)**. For those of us who are born again, what is more important is that our bodies must be kept holy. The lord's second coming will be for a pure, holy and unblemished church.

I came to the deep realization that if my body was a temple of the Holy Spirit.

This meant I must completely shake off the desires of my flesh;

The acts of the flesh are obvious; sexual immorality, impurity and debauchery; idolatry and witchcraft, hatred, discord, jealousy, fits of rage, selfish ambition, dissensions, factions and envy, drunkenness, orgies and the like..
Galatians 5; 19

And embrace the fruits of the Spirit as mentioned in
Galatians 5:22

Jackson Odeny Oyoo;   Memories of my life.

The fruit of the Spirit is Love, Joy, Peace, Forbearance, Kindness, Goodness, faithfulness, Gentleness and Self-control. Against such things there is no law.

4.   The meaning of Salvation in my life

Body, Soul and Spirit

Some issues were becoming clearer to me by the day. Before I was born again, I had the fallen Adam nature, with no spirit of God inside me. I will explain.

When God molded Adam out of mud **(Genesis 2; 7),** He breathed into Adam's lifeless body the breath of life. Adam became a living soul with the spirit of God inside him. He was, in other words, a total human being with Body, Soul and Spirit. God also created out of Adam's rib a helper, called Eve. He then gave Adam the power to control the earthly creation (everything including animals and plants) except for one thing, the tree in the middle of the garden, the tree of the knowledge of good and evil, for God said,

' You are free to eat from any tree in the garden, but you must not eat from the tree of the knowledge of good and evil, for when you eat from it you will certainly die' **Genesis 2; 16**

But Adam was cheated into eating the forbidden fruit by the influence of his wife Eve, through the snake (**Genesis chapter 3**). As this was against God's instruction, the lord God removed his spirit from Adam and cursed the ground from which he ate the forbidden fruit. So Adam became a living soul with no spirit of God. He instantly became, although physically alive for many years, spiritually dead upon disobeying God's command. The descendants of Adam, all of us, are by nature spiritually dead on birth, hence our cravings for fleshly desires upon birth. I realized this was the state under which I was operating before I knew God. In other words I was born in sin, with soul and fleshly desires. No spirit of God was found in me. When I became born again I instantly became a living soul with the spirit of God inside me.

I will again explain what this means to me:

As man allows the spirit of God in his life, the body and soul are enjoined by the spirit and man passes from spiritual death to life. In the end I became convinced that the Spirit, soul and body have different but interrelated functions, summarized as follows:

Jackson Odeny Oyoo;   Memories of my life.

1. The spirit: God conscious, the unseen part which becomes conscious of God's eternal power.

2. The soul: self-conscious, the unseen part, what comprises the personality of the human being; the mind, the emotions, the will and the intelligence.

3. The body: world conscious, what the physical eyes are able to see; the eye, nose, ear, head, brain, stomach, and any other body organ. It is the vessel which is used by the soul.

5. **The power of the Cross, passing over from death to life.**

The significance of the death of Jesus Christ on the cross became clearer as I progressively fixed my eyes on Jesus. The provisions for our eternal redemption were already made in heaven even before the Lord walked on earth. Isaiah had already prophesized many centuries earlier. The provisions were already there before the time Jesus was nailed on the cross and resurrected with power.

Isaiah 53

Who has believed our message and to whom has the arm of the Lord been revealed....

Jackson Odeny Oyoo;   Memories of my life.

He had no beauty or majesty to attract us to him,

Nothing in his appearance that we should desire him

He was despised and rejected by mankind,

A man of many suffering and familiar with pain,

Like one from whom people hide their faces,

He was despised and we held him in low esteem

Surely he took up our pain

And bore our suffering,

Yet we considered him punished by God,

And stricken by him, and afflicted.

But he was pierced for our transgressions,

He was crushed for our iniquities,

The punishment that bore us peace was on him,

And by his wounds we were healed

We all, like sheep, have gone astray,

Jackson Odeny Oyoo;   Memories of my life.

Each of us has turned to our own way;

And the lord has laid on him the iniquity of us all………
(Read through the whole chapter)

With a spiritual insight I now understood that the significance of the cross lay in its power of crossing over from death, just like Jesus did when he was nailed to death through the cross, but rose from the dead on the third day with power, and gave his authority to those who accepted him by faith. Whatever they bound on earth using his name was bound in heaven. Paul says

> *'May I never boast except in the cross of our lord Jesus Christ, through which the world has been crucified to me and I to the world'.* **Galatians 6; 14**

> *'For the message of the cross is foolishness to those who are perishing, but to us who are being saved it is the power of God'* **1 Corinthians 1; 18**

Jackson Odeny Oyoo; Memories of my life.

6. The Subconscious Mind; the battle ground for transformation of the whole self

As far as I was concerned the seat of the battle in me was in the control of my subconscious mind.

I learnt that whoever and whatever controlled my subconscious mind controlled my heart. We have the choice to allow our souls to be controlled by Satan or by God.

Our Lord said

A good man brings good things out the good stored up in his heart, and an evil man brings evil things out of the evil stored up in his heart. For the mouth speaks what the heart is full of. **Luke 6:45**

Repetitive action on the issues we hear with our ears, see with our eyes, touch and feel with our bodies form our habits. At first they are in our outer conscious minds, not dangerous enough. But doing them repetitively downloads them into our inner minds, the subconscious mind. Once there, they run without our awareness just like a computer; what is visible on the screen is made up of what has been installed in the software, silently working behind the scenes.

Jackson Odeny Oyoo;   Memories of my life.

Either they become very useful or very dangerous. That is why the subconscious mind is the most important part of a human being. What is stored inside the soul through the mind determines the character of the person, even the destiny of the person. Only through a complete transformation of the soul and body by accepting the spirit of God can one's mind be renewed to conform to the image of our Lord and savior, Jesus Christ.

Therefore if any man be in Christ, he is a new creature: Old things are passed away, behold all things are become new. **2nd Corinthians 5; 17**.

When we accept the Lord into our lives and fix our minds to the teachings in the Holy Bible and on Jesus Christ, a complete transformation takes place. We give up our souls for Christ and internalize his teachings, the word of God into our hearts.

This is what happened to me.

7.   Covenant with my legs, eyes, mouth and ears

I made a covenant with my heart to give God my total self in order to be safe. To me this implied that my legs, eyes, ears, mouth and total self should focus only on the things which glorify the name of God and not the things of the world or the devil. A good example is the kind of videos one watches e.g. phonography and other love videos; the companies one keeps as friends; the places one goes to and the matters which delight one's heart, as in Psalms Chapter 1, thus

> *'Blessed is the one who does not walk in step with the wicked or stand in the way that sinners take or sit in the company of mockers, but whose delight is in the law of the LORD, and who meditates on his law day and night. That person is like a tree planted by streams of water, which yields its fruit in season and whose leaf does not wither- whatever he does prospers''*

I always ask myself whether what I am thinking, what I speak or what I intend to do will glorify God. I rely on the Holy Book

Jackson Odeny Oyoo;   Memories of my life.

to teach me to behold what is beautiful in the eyes of God, thus

> **Exodus 15;26** *If you listen carefully to the lord your God and do what is right in His eyes, if you pay attention to his commands and keep all his decrees, I will not bring on you any of the diseases I brought on the Egyptians, for I am the LORD, who heals you.*

> **Deuteronomy 12;28** *Be careful to obey all these regulations I am giving you, so that it may always go well with you, and your children after you, because you will be doing what is good and right in the eyes of the Lord your God..*

The holy book has always impressed into me repeatedly to live by the Holy Spirit in order not to gratify the desires of my flesh.

> *So I say, walk by the spirit, and you will not gratify the desires of the flesh.* **Galatians 5; 16.**

Jackson Odeny Oyoo;   Memories of my life.

8. The significance the blood of Jesus Christ, the forgiveness and cleansing of sin

I began to understand that our redemption, our sanctification, the destruction of the power of Satan in our lives is only through the proclamation of the blood of Jesus Christ.

I regretted the use of animal blood over satanic sicknesses which had been caused on my life through witchcraft, yet there was already a provision through the redemptive blood of our Lord.

In the Old Testament, God the father directed the sprinkling of the blood of sacrificed year old lambs, without defects, on the sides and tops of the doors of all Israelites in Egypt during the Passover night. This would spare them from death when the God's Angel of death passed at night to kill the first born sons of the Egyptians (Exodus 12). An analogy of this demonstrates the importance of blood in human life. Even in African communities animal blood sacrifices were and are still used in some cultures to sanctify community or individual sins. Nevertheless these sacrifices must be

Jackson Odeny Oyoo;   Memories of my life.

undertaken periodically because they are not able to permanently clear our consciences from all sin.

In Hebrews Chapter 9, we are told that when Christ came for the good things which are already here, he went through the more perfect tabernacle, not made of human hands. He did not enter by the sprinkling of human blood, but once and for all with his own blood, thus obtaining eternal redemption for all humanity.

This blood, when proclaimed, destroys the power of sin and cancels the curses in our lives. The one thing that Satan cannot face eternally is the holy blood of Jesus Christ.

The blood of Jesus Christ therefore eternally sanctified me from all sins. I was no longer my own but a child of God through sanctification.

> *The blood of goats and bulls and the ashes of of a heifer sprinkled on those who are ceremonially unclean sanctify them so that they are outwardly clean. How much more, then, will the blood of Christ, who through the eternal spirit offered himself unblemished to God, cleanse our consciences from acts that lead to death, so that we may serve the living God?*

Jackson Odeny Oyoo;   Memories of my life.

For this reason Christ is the mediator of a new covenant, that those who are called may receive the promised eternal inheritance – now that he has died as ransom to set them free from the sins committed under the first covenant. **Hebrews Chapter 9; 13..**

By prayer and groaning every morning I began to proclaim the blood of Jesus over myself, over my family members and came to believe by faith that my proclamations were coming to pass.

Through the blood of Jesus, I was redeemed out of the hand of Satan.

- Through the blood of Jesus, all my sins were forgiven. The blood of Jesus cleansed me from all sins.
- Through the blood of Jesus, I was justified, made righteous, just-as-if-I'd never sinned.
- Through the blood of Jesus, I was sanctified, made holy, set apart to God. I am no longer in Satan's territory

Jackson Odeny Oyoo;   Memories of my life.

9.   The root cause of the curses in my life and their removal

Since I came from an unknown root I may have been an heir to a curse that may be compared to a weed planted in my life, linking me to satanic forces outside myself. This weed had two kinds of roots: one long tap root going straight downward, and other less powerful lateral roots stretching out in various directions.

The tap root represented the influence of my ancestors who might have worshiped false gods and practiced witchcraft. I was told that one of our fore fathers in our Oyoo sub clan, was the anointed one among the Gem Rae clan to undertake ceremonial cleansing of the clan, and this he performed by the use of snakes and other paraphernalia. The story goes on to this day that without his cleansing activities, Gem Rae would not have survived. As far as I was concerned this was a generational curse which followed members of this clan to date.

The lateral roots of my ancestral tree represented other influences to which I was exposed in my own lifetime, either through various sins I committed or through my own

Jackson Odeny Oyoo;   Memories of my life.

attachment to false gods or in various other ways. I thought my occasional visit to Legio Maria cult was a direct provocation to God, because what they preached and practiced was not in consonance with the word in the Holy bible and what the Lord preached. For instance digging a wall to fetch paraphernalia by members of Legio Maria or other forms of witchcraft was not compatible with the lord's walk on earth.

The book of Proverbs and Deuteronomy is full of curses which could have befallen me and likewise my siblings. These were.

o   I was taken into the captivity of alcoholism, sexual sin and disobedience to God. Countless parents in the present generation have experienced this curse. They have seen their sons and daughters taken captive by a rebellious subculture devoted to drugs, sex, satanic music and every form of the occult.

"You shall beget sons and daughters, but they shall not be yours; for they shall go into captivity." **Deuteronomy 28:41**

Jackson Odeny Oyoo; Memories of my life.

o   I suffered lack. Whatever I received in the form of monthly salary was consumed through careless living, not caring about the survival of my mother and my family members.

"Because you did not serve the LORD your God with joy and gladness of heart, for the abundance of everything, therefore you shall serve your enemies, whom the LORD will send against you, in hunger, in thirst, in nakedness, and in need of everything." **Det. 28; Verses 47–48:**

o   As far as I was I had neither the material riches nor the spiritual riches. I was totally depraved of happiness and good health,

"There is one who makes himself rich, yet has nothing; and one who makes himself poor, yet has great riches." **Proverbs 13:7**

o   I realized that the form of disobedience that most surely and inevitably provoked God's curse upon anybody's life, mine included, was the breaking of the first two of the Ten Commandments,

Jackson Odeny Oyoo;   Memories of my life.

"I am the LORD your God, who brought you out of the land of Egypt, out of the house of bondage. You shall have no other gods before me. You shall not make for yourself a carved image—any likeness of anything that is in heaven above, or that is in the earth beneath, or that is in the water under the earth; You shall not bow down to them nor serve them. For I, the LORD your God, am a jealous God, visiting the iniquity of the fathers upon the children to the third and fourth generations of those who hate Me." **Exodus 20:1–5**

For although they knew God, they neither glorified him as God nor gave thanks to him, but their thinking became futile and their foolish hearts were darkened. Although they claimed to be wise, they became fools and exchanged the glory of the immortal God for images made to look like mortal man and birds and animals and reptiles. **Romans 1:20–23**

It became clear to me that the true God, revealed first in creation and then more fully in Scripture, is holy, awesome, glorious, and omnipotent. To represent Him in the likeness of any created being—whether human or animal—is to offer

Jackson Odeny Oyoo; Memories of my life.

Him a deliberate insult. It is a calculated provocation of His wrath. Breaking of the first two commandments bears the characteristic mark of a curse: It continues from generation to generation, at least as far as the fourth generation.

Before I could enjoy true liberty and the fullness of the new creation in Christ, this weed needed to be completely pulled out, with all its roots. The most important root, and the one hardest to deal with, was the tap root that may have linked me to many generations who have worshiped false gods.

Nothing but the supernatural grace and power of God could effectively remove all the roots. But thank God, there was hope in the promise of Jesus in **Matthew 15:13***"Every plant which my heavenly Father has not planted will be uprooted."*

I stand here to renounce all these curses in the name of Jesus Christ. By the power of the blood of Jesus I proclaim the replacement of these curses with the blessings of the God of Abraham, Isaac and Jacob.

We have to understand that full provision for the nullification of all the curses has already been made through the death of Jesus on the Cross. That's the way God has made for the provision for every human need including release from a curse. *"Christ has redeemed us from the curse of the law, having become a curse for us (for it is written, 'Cursed is everyone who hangs on a tree'), that the blessing of Abraham might come upon the Gentiles in Christ Jesus, that we might receive the promise of the Spirit through faith."* **(Galatians 3:13, 14)**

The death of Jesus on the cross, the atonement, was the exchange in which all the evil due to us came upon Christ; that all the good due to Him might be made available to us. He was wounded that we might be healed. He died that we might have life. He was made sin that we might be made righteous. He was rejected that we might be accepted. In particular, He was made a curse that we might enter into the blessing. The provisions were already made by God as in **Isaiah 53.**

CHAPTER 9

LIVING IN THE KINGDOM OF GOD.

As far as I know living in the Kingdom of God is spiritual. There are two spiritual kingdoms which oppose one another; The Kingdom of light with Jesus Christ given all authority by God to be the head and the kingdom of darkness with Satan as the head.

1. Exercising the authority of our Lord Jesus Christ

With salvation I found myself placed in God's kingdom, a kingdom eternal not ruled by men and women but by God, with Jesus Christ given all authority in heaven and on earth. The same authority was extended to me, to be exercised in the name of Jesus Christ.

Jesus said,

'All authority in heaven and in earth has been given to me. Therefore go and make disciples of all nations, baptizing them in the name of the Father, the son and the Holy Spirit and teaching them to obey everything I have commanded you.'

Mathews 28; 18

It was now clear to me that only God has absolute authority, and that this authority is delegated to his only begotten son Jesus Christ. That all other forms of authority were subject to limitations of various kinds, was not in dispute. Delegated authority is valid only within a given sphere. For instance a ruler's authority is limited by the laws of his nation and does not extend to "private" areas in the lives of his subjects. A father's authority over his family does not permit him to infringe upon the laws of the government. A teacher has authority over his pupils only within the limits of school life. A pastor has authority over his congregation only in matters that are governed by their denomination.

The Lord has given clear directions how the authority he gave his disciples is to to be exercised. We who have been in grafted into God's kingdom through the cross have also become the disciples of Jesus Christ. We have accepted him as our Lord and savior.

Jesus said *'You know that the rulers of the gentiles lord it over them, and their high officials exercise authority over them. Not so with you. Whoever wants to become great among you must be your servant, and whoever wants to be first must be your slave, just as the son of man did not come to be served ,*

Jackson Odeny Oyoo;   Memories of my life.

but to serve, and to give his life as a ransom for many'.
Mathews 20; 25

I came to the deep realization that the authority that was in me meant that I was a servant of my fellow Christians and a slave of the lord, following the lord's voice in earnest. This was the actual life in the Kingdom, to follow the voice of God, the voice of Jesus Christ.

Jesus Christ is the only authority I have which will give me all directions of life. Everything I do must be for the glory of God. We who were far away have been in grafted into God's Kingdom by Jesus Christ. He laid down his life for this purpose, that the Gentiles may also be his sheep. The Lord says in **John 10; 14-17.**

> *I am the good shepherd; and I know my sheep and am known by my own. As the father knows me, even so I know the father; and I lay down my life for the sheep and other sheep I have which are not of this fold; them also I must bring, and they will hear my voice, and there will be one flock and one shepherd. Therefore my father loves me, because I lay down my life that I may take it again.*

Jackson Odeny Oyoo;   Memories of my life.

2.   Gentiles (me included) now in grafted into God's Kingdom.

We, the gentiles who were far away from the promises of God to Abraham have been in grafted through the shading of the blood of Jesus on the cross. We are now equal partakers of the promise, which were originally availed to Israel only.

'Remember that you were at that time separated from Christ, alienated from the Commonwealth of Israel and strangers to the covenant of promise, having no hope and without God in the world.

But now in Christ Jesus you who were once far off have been brought near by the blood of Jesus.

For He himself is our peace, who has made us both one and has broken down in his flesh the dividing wall of hostility'.
Ephesians 2; 12 -14

3.   The blessings of Abraham

Abraham is the only person of human descent through which the promises of God were passed: **Genesis 12; 1-3**

The lord said to Abram 'Go from your country, your people and your father's household to the land I will show you

I will make you a great nation, and I will bless you; I will make your name great, and you will be a blessing.

I will bless those who bless you, and who ever curses you I will curse; and all peoples on earth will be blessed through you.

Abraham obeyed God, hence he is the father of our faith.

The blessings which Moses proclaimed to the people of Israel were in accordance to the promise given by God to Abraham and are fully expressed in **Deuteronomy 28; 1-14, excerpts**

If you obey the Lord your God and carefully follow all his commandments I give you today, the Lord your God will set you high above the Nations of the earth

The Lord will establish you as His holy people, as he promised you on oath, if you keep the commands of the Lord your God and walk in obedience to him

Then all the peoples of the earth will see that you are called by the name of the Lord and they will fear you

The lord will grant you abundant prosperity- in the fruit of your womb, the young of your livestock and the crops of your ground- in the land he swore your ancestors to give you

The Lord will make you the head and not the tail... (The head makes decisions, the tail follows)

These are the blessings which have been extended to us the Gentiles by the death of our Lord on the cross. They are still in accordance with the promise given to Abraham that 'all *peoples on earth will be blessed through you'*.

The blessings of Abraham are now embodied in the spiritual blessings.

The blessings were originally physical and depended on the obedience to the Ten Commandments given by Moses. Through the death of Jesus Christ on the cross, we became

Jackson Odeny Oyoo;   Memories of my life.

partakers of the blessings of God which were now transited from the physical realms to the tablets of our hearts.

The lord gave a clear direction on how to tap into all the blessings of God, thus

> *Seek first His kingdom and His righteousness, and all these things will be given to you as well* **Mathews 6; 33**

For me seeking the Kingdom of God involves seeking God by praying earnestly every morning and walking by the Spirit every day. We are no longer directed by the Law of the Ten Commandments but by the spirit of God stamped on our hearts, which gives us the righteousness to live within the law. The manifestation of the fruits of the Holy Spirit requires no written law.

> *You show that you are a letter from Christ, the result of our ministry, written not with ink but with the spirit of the living God, not on tablets of stone but on tablets of human hearts.* **2 Corinthians 3; 3**

> *Walk by the Spirit, and you will not gratify the desires of the flesh, for the flesh desires what is contrary to the spirit, and the spirit what is contrary to the flesh. They are in*

conflict with each other, so that you are not to do whatever you want. **Galatians 5; 16.**

4. Tapping into the blessings of the Lord through His promises at the Sermon on the Mount.

In the book of **Mathews chapter 5,** The lord promises the following blessings to the obedient;

Verse 3: When we recognize that we are poor spiritually, he will rescue us from this poverty by giving us the riches in His glory.

Verse 4: When we mourn over our sins, the lord will comforts us as we repent.

Verse 5: When we walk in meekness, we are assured of inheriting all places we go to as we proclaim salvation to unbelievers.

Verse 6: As we hunger and thirst for righteousness we are filled by the Holy Spirit

Jackson Odeny Oyoo; Memories of my life.

Verse 7: As we show mercy we in return receive the Lord's mercy

Verse 8: The purity of the heart is an assurance of seeing God

Verse 9: The peacemakers shall be called children of God. We will be the salt of the earth.

Verse 10: Those who are persecuted and called all manner of names because of righteousness and because of the Lord's name should rejoice, for great is their reward in heaven.

My every desire is to tap into these blessings through trusting and obeying the voice of the Lord.

5. Producing the fruits of the Holy Spirit in the Kingdom.

These are well expressed by Paul in Galatians 5:22-24. As we live in the Kingdom of God which came by Jesus Christ, we are expected to produce the fruits of the Holy Spirit:

Jackson Odeny Oyoo;   Memories of my life.

KJV; But *the fruit of the Spirit is* **love, joy, peace, longsuffering, faith, meekness, temperance;** *against such there is no law. And they that are Christ's have crucified the flesh with the affections and lusts.*

The manifestation of these spiritual fruits marked my victory in the walk with Christ. I will explain how;

i.   Love

Being my Shepherd, the Lord has always filled my heart with unconditional love. There were times that I held so much unforgiveness in my heart that in most times they were reflected in my erratic behavior.

But thanks be to The King of glory and the lord of my righteousness. He made me to

- Forgive all my Aunts, particularly my younger Aunt who had inflicted pain on me in my youthful years

- Forgive my siblings. Satan tempted me to remind them of all the help I had given them to bring them up, yet they did not care about me particularly when I lost my job. They did not come to my aid even when my children were missing school because of lack of school fees. I forgave them unconditionally.

- o Forgive the friends who deserted me when I lost my formal employment because of my shortcomings.

- o Forgive all people who had trespassed against me in one way or the other.

The lord filled me with the love attributes of forgiveness without holding grudges. I always have the mind of peace that emanates from this forgiveness attribute and walk in humility. The following words gave me great strength:

Nothing makes the heart pure
And gives an everlasting cure
Than this heavenly act of forgiving
It is a priceless gift in living
Yet it involves nothing
But silently counts on everything
It turns foes into great friends

Jackson Odeny Oyoo;   Memories of my life.

And fills their hearts with love that God sends

Where granted a seed is sown

Where received reigns a sense of peace that's never

known

For forgiveness is but a piece from heaven

With it the world is a love haven

This love, what our lord directs as the second greatest commandment *'love your neighbor as yourself'* Mathew **22;39**, is well expounded by Paul, and now internalized by me

Love is patient, love is kind. It does not envy, it does not boast, it is not proud

It is not rude. It is not self-seeking. It is not easily angered. It keeps no record of wrongs

Love does not delight in evil but rejoices with the truth

It always protects, always trusts, always hopes, always perseveres

1st Corinthians 13

Jackson Odeny Oyoo;   Memories of my life.

I came to know that one can only reach the state of unconditional love when one crucifies the fleshly desires on the cross and allows the spirit of God to take over one's life, the acquisition of the righteousness of God.

The righteousness I live is not righteousness of my own, but a righteousness which comes with the saving power of our Lord, just as Paul says

'This righteousness is given through faith in Jesus Christ to all who believe. There is no difference between the Jew and the Gentile'. **Romans 3; 22** and elsewhere **in Romans 6, 16,** *'you have been set free from sin and become slaves to righteousness* and in **Romans 10;4,** *Christ is the culmination of the law so that there may be righteousness for everyone who believes.* This righteousness is all summarized in **2 Corinthians 5; 21** that *God made him who had no sin to be sin for us, so that in him we might become the righteousness of God.*

But a word of caution, this love does not mean we should yoke together with non-believers for Paul warns in **2 Corinthians 6:14,** *'Do not be yoked together with non-*

Jackson Odeny Oyoo;   Memories of my life.

believers. For what do righteousness and wickedness have in common? Or what fellowship can light have with darkness?

ii.   Joy

The joy I have in Christ does not depend on the state of my happiness, gladness, sadness, sorrows or pain. All these are momentary.

It stands out on its own and is constant irrespective of any dispositional circumstances. It is a result of rejoicing in the power or might of the Lord, looking at what the Lord has done in my life. It is rejoicing with the truth. Paul says in the book of Philippians 4; 4 *'Rejoice in the Lord always. I will say it again Rejoice'.*

He repeats the word 'rejoice' more than 15 times in the book of Philippians.

One thing I have gone through and learnt from Paul is that I will remain contented and rejoice in every situation, even in the dark moments. Like Paul I say,

Jackson Odeny Oyoo; Memories of my life.

I have learned to be content whatever the circumstances. I know what it is to be in need, and I know what it is to have plenty. I have learned the secret of being content in every circumstance, whether well fed or hungry.

I can do all things through Christ who strengthens me.
(Philippians Chapter 4).

And this has been the secret of my joy. To me rejoicing means that I am not my own. I belong to Jesus Christ. He purchased me with his blood, and it no longer I who lives but Christ in me. Because of this I can do all things through Christ who strengthens me,

I will rejoice with the Lord because he has clothed me with the garments of salvation and put in me a robe of righteousness

*I delight greatly in the Lord, my soul **rejoices** in my God. For He has clothed me with garments of salvation and arrayed me in a robe of righteousness; as a bridegroom adorns his head like a priest, and as a bride adorns herself with her jewels.**(Isaiah 61; 10)***

Jackson Odeny Oyoo;   Memories of my life.

I will be glad and rejoice in your love, for you saw my affliction and knew the anguish of my soul. **(Psalms 31; 7)**

I will rejoice for I am assured my name is written in the Lambs book of life

However, do not rejoice that the spirits submit to you, but rejoice that your names are written in heaven **Luke 10; 20**

I will rejoice in the Lord for the great things he has done in my life. I will rejoice in the Lord always, for he cares for me

Cast all your anxiety on him for He cares for you **1 Peter 5; 7**

I will rejoice in the lord always for he has allowed me to sing praises in his name

Sing to God, sing in praise of his name; extol him who rises on the clouds; rejoice before him- his name is The Lord. **(Psalms 68; 4)**

Jackson Odeny Oyoo;   Memories of my life.

I will rejoice in the lord always, for he has clothed me with meekness

The meek also shall increase their joy in Jehovah, and the poor among men shall rejoice in the holy one of Israel. **(Isaiah 29; 19)**

Let me hear joy and gladness; let the bones you have crushed rejoice. **(Psalms 51; 8)**

iii.   Peace

Peace from God, Peace of God and Peace with God

I made peace with myself the day I surrendered my life to the Lord. Previously I had no peace, only chasing after the whirl winds i.e.

Chasing after women, who were only interested in my money and breaking my marriage. Frequent sleep outs gave me no peace with my wives.

Chasing after alcohol from bar to bar until my pockets were empty, consuming all to the drink. No plans worked. All the plans which involved money never worked for me.

Jackson Odeny Oyoo;   Memories of my life.

Chasing after money through acts of corruption. The money never helped me because it went the same way it came; abrupt.

Chasing after pride and arrogance because of my misplaced position brought about by education, seniority in jobs. In the end pride consumed me. I became a toothless bulldog in the society after I lost formal employment.

I kept on chasing and chasing after these winds until when the lord came into my life and put a stop. I now had a peace of mind that surpassed my understanding. I began not to lean on my own understanding in all things that happened to me, except to focus on God. The Lord gave me

Peace with my wives

Peace without chasing after money

Peace with my enemies. I no longer pursued the line that some were my enemies and some were not. I made peace with everybody.

In other words I made peace with myself and I found myself with no grudge with anybody.

Jackson Odeny Oyoo;   Memories of my life.

I was no I longer a friend of Satan. I completely let my soul go off satanic activities like witchcraft 1and bowing down to false gods; believing that I had to somehow worship some people in order to receive favor from them; doing occult with some denominations which were devilish in their practices.

In other words I decided to unequivocally seek God, experience Him in my life and surrender my soul to Him. God the father, God the Son and God the Holy Ghost came into my soul. There was no longer any room to play with the Almighty. So I became a living soul with the spirit of God in me. I started living in the fear of God (*The fear of God that is wisdom. Shunning evil that is understanding.* **(Job 28; 28))**, and started living at peace with Him and with all people.

Henceforth I followed God's word concerning the desire for peace with God and peace with fellow man, as I heard from His voice, thus

> *Submit to God and be at **peace** with him, in this way prosperity will come to you* **(Job 22; 21)**

> *The Lord gives strength to His people; The Lord blesses his people with peace* **(Psalms 20; 11)**

Jackson Odeny Oyoo;   Memories of my life.

The meek will inherit the land and enjoy peace and prosperity **(Psalms 37; 11)**

Of wisdom: Her ways are pleasant ways and her paths are peace **(Proverbs 3; 17)**

A heart at peace gives life to the bones, but envy rots the bones **(Proverbs 14; 30)**

Better a dry crust with peace and quiet than a house full of feasting and strife **(Proverbs 17; 1)**

Discipline your children, and they will give you peace; they will bring you the delights you desire **(Proverbs 29; 17)**

Peace I leave with you; my peace I give you. I do not give you as the world gives. Do not let your hearts be troubled and do not be afraid. **(John 14; 27)**

Jackson Odeny Oyoo; Memories of my life.

*For the Kingdom of God is not matter of eating and drinking, but of righteousness, peace and joy in the Holy Spirit.***(Romans 14;17)**

And the peace of God, which transcends all understanding, will guard your hearts and your minds in Christ Jesus **(Philippians 4; 7)**

iv.   Long suffering

Long suffering embodies the following:

- o **Patience**   To be still before the Lord and wait patiently for him **(Psalms 37; 7)**
- o **Endurance** Inspired by hope in our Lord Jesus Christ **(Thessalonians 1; 3)**
- o **Perseverance.** To finish its work that we may be mature and complete, not lacking anything (**James 1; 4**)
- o **Persistence**   To those who by persistence in doing good seek glory, honor and immortality He will give eternal life **(Romans 2; 7)**

Whatever I do, I do for the sake of Christ so that the glory of the Lord is revealed. Whether it is patience when I am

Jackson Odeny Oyoo; Memories of my life.

slapped and feel like heartbroken, enduring hardship in an unfavorable environment, persevering consistently despite failure to achieve a goal, persisting in calling my brother to Christ even though he keeps turning me down. All these will turn into joy when the Kingdom of God is revealed, when the desired results come to fruition.

The capacity to translate vision into reality, to influence people to realize beneficial aspirations demands long suffering. To me, it demands total sacrifice, giving up certain things for the purpose of gaining later. It calls for service without the appreciation of other people but only for the sake of Christ, what Paul says in **Colossians 3;23**

> *Whatever you do, work at it with all your heart, as working for the lord, not for human masters*

Achieving solutions, means that I have to be focused, must have a sound balance of the daily pressures I face with clarity of purpose. I must be simple in my approach to life. All these characteristics are embodied in longsuffering.

Jackson Odeny Oyoo;   Memories of my life.

In order to catch up with the spirit of leadership, I am always ready to be transformed through training and servitude, what the lord said

Follow me, and I will make you fishers of men **Mark 1; 17**

Whoever wants to be my disciple must deny themselves and take up their cross and follow me **Mark 8:34**

I am the light of the world. Whoever follows me will never walk in darkness, but will have the light of life **John 8; 12**

Therefore longsuffering is a call which demands denial of many things of life, accepting to follow Jesus unconditionally and walking in the light given by the Lord.

v.   Gentleness,

Everything in gentleness is in the inner spiritual mind not the outward adornment. Modest outward appearance is good, but should not under all circumstances take over from the gentleness experienced from the inner self.

I aspire this to be my overriding value in importance, because without gentleness there is no humility, unconditional love

Jackson Odeny Oyoo;   Memories of my life.

cannot come to fore and longsuffering becomes unbearable. What Peter said is applicable to all sexes:

Your beauty should not come from outward adornment, such as elaborate hairstyles and the wearing of gold jewelry or fine clothes. Rather it should be that of your inner self, the unfading beauty of a gentle and quiet spirit, which is of great worth **1 Peter 3-4.**

The unfading beauty of a gentle and quiet spirit is translated in the way we talk with one another in our relationships all directions, whether at family level, at friendship level, in business and even in the way we handle people who consider us their enemies. Here the tongue is of great importance, we must watch out our tongues

For me to gain gentleness and a quiet spirit, I desire:

- o   Words of wisdom to come from my mouth and to speak what is just.

   The mouths of the righteous utter wisdom, and their tongues speak what is just **Psalms 37; 30**

Jackson Odeny Oyoo;   Memories of my life.

o   To dwell in the secret places of the Lord to be one whose talk is blameless and to speak the truth from my heart so that there is no slander in me.

Lord who may dwell in your sacred tent? Who may live in your holy mountain? The one whose talk is blameless, who does what is righteous, who speaks the truth from their hearts, whose tongue utters no slander, who does no wrong to a neighbor, and casts no slur on others **Psalms 15;1-**

Those who guard their mouths and their tongues keep themselves from calamity **Proverbs 21; 23**

o   To encourage the weary by the words which come from my mouth.

The sovereign lord has given me a well instructed tongue, to know the word that sustains the weary. He wakens me morning by morning, wakens my ear to listen like one being instructed **Isaiah 50; 4**

Jackson Odeny Oyoo;   Memories of my life.

o   To guard my tongue always, aware that it may corrupt my whole body and because it is a vessel also used by the devil

The tongue is also a fire, a world of evil among the parts of the body. It corrupts the whole body, sets the whole course on one's life on fire, and is itself set on fire by hell **James 3;6**

*Whoever would love life and see good days must keep their tongue from evil and their lips from deceitful speech.***1 Peter 3;10**

vi.   Goodness

I have tasted the goodness of the lord. He had mercy on me, and brought me with his mighty hands from the Kingdom of darkness to his glorious Kingdom of light. Oh yes, the Lord is ever merciful, ever gracious and ever faithful. I proclaim his goodness in all ways every morning when I wake u

It is because of his goodness that

o   He gave his begotten son to mankind as a ransom for the sins of many **John 3;16**

Jackson Odeny Oyoo;   Memories of my life.

o He has mercy on whomever he has mercy and compassion on   whomever he has compassion **Exodus 33;19**

o He allows his elect to eat to the full and become well-nourished **Nehemiah 9;25**

o He allows goodness and love to follow his elect all the days of their lives **Psalm 23;**

vii.   Faith

Faith is calling on the things that are not as though they are, in the mighty name of Jesus, and they come to pass. Faith is what has sustained me in the very difficult seasons of my life.

Through faith I have endured I have persisted, I have waited patiently for the Lord. Never disappointing, he has always revealed himself to me. That is why I proclaim, every morning, parts of Psalm 23 upon my life, in my own words, and by faith that:

The Lord is my shepherd, I will not lack, I will not fear

Jackson Odeny Oyoo; *Memories of my life.*

He makes me sleep in green pastures; He provides me with the desires of my heart

He makes me walk beside quiet waters; He is my righteousness, my peace

Yes, even though I find myself sometimes walking in the valley of the shadow of death, I will not fear, because I know that the lord is with me in the valley

He prepares a table for me right in the presence of my enemies

My very cup overflows with love, joy and peace

The Lord has anointed me to preach his word in season and out of season

Surely the mercies of the lord, the love of God, fellowshipping with the Holy Spirit shall be my portion all the days of my life

And my soul will dwell in the house of the Lord forever

I have in the course of my salvation observed and experienced that

Jackson Odeny Oyoo;   Memories of my life.

o	Faith is the shield with which to extinguish the arrows of the evil one, the powers of the enemies in the heavenly realms, the persons without bodies hovering around our midst. The only thing that demons fear is the name of Jesus and the blood of Jesus.

o	Faith is the supplier of my needs in accordance with riches in God's glory. I do not worry about my daily bread and my very genuine needs because I know the Lord will give. How He does it is his own way, because everything belongs to him. He is an all sufficient God and everything is for His glory.

o	Faith is a sword through which the word of God reaches the sick, the poor, the rich, the heavily burdened and the worried. All burdens were lifted at Calvary. The provisions of God are already there. All we need is to proclaim them by faith.

o	Faith is the means by which we are brought out of darkness into the light of God. Through faith we are made righteous and our righteousness is reflected in what and the way we talk, what we put on as our clothing, the people we associate with, our daily behavior. Do we live and rejoice with the truth? That is what we should ask ourselves always.

Faith is everything **(Hebrews 11).** If we want to live in peace, in love and joy, we must embrace faith, not leaning on our understanding but on every word that proceeds from the mouth of God. The word of God is already revealed in his Holy Books and by **the** Holy Spirit.

viii.   Meekness

Meekness is a virtue characterized by humility, non-boastfulness, modesty, and submission to God's will upon our lives. I realize that committed Christians have the potential for the good of our nation, the good of our societies and the good of our families.

The Bible places the responsibility of humility upon us. It is not an emotion, but the surrendering of our souls in total submission to God. Why the soul? Because it is our ego, which part always says 'I'. This is the barrier which brings self-centeredness. It is the barrier which must be brought to the subjection of God, and can only be broken by surrendering our souls to God in total humility.

Jackson Odeny Oyoo; Memories of my life.

The bible gives a clear condition for God's healing of the nations, even from the family level.

If my people, who are called by my name, will humble themselves and pray and seek my face and turnaround from their wicked ways, then I will hear from heaven, and I will forgive their sins and will heal their land

2nd Chronicles 7; 14

Total subjection of the soul to humility brings first, wisdom, then respect, honor and even the good things we desire to have. My prayer always is to surrender my

- Appetite for violence
- Haughty eyes
- Perverse lips
- Selfish ambition

So that I am able to acquire through humility

- The fear of God
- The grace of God
- Wisdom and understanding
- Riches spiritual and satisfaction with what the lord has allowed me to have

Jackson Odeny Oyoo;   Memories of my life.

Respect and honor upwards and downwards i.e. from my elders, my peers and the people below me, putting high values on others before me

And these qualities are God given.

But the meek will inherit the earth and enjoy peace and prosperity **Psalms 37; 11**

Blessed are the meek, for they will inherit the earth **Mathews 5; 5**

Before a downfall the heart is haughty but humility comes before honor. **Proverbs 18; 12**

Humility is the fear of God, its wages are riches, honor and life **Proverbs 22; 4**

Who is wise and understanding among you? Let them show it by their good life, by deeds done in the humility that comes with wisdom **James 3; 13**

In the same way, you who are younger, submit yourselves to your elders. All of you clothe yourselves with humility towards one another, because God

Jackson Odeny Oyoo;   Memories of my life.

opposes the proud but shows favor to the humble **1 Peter 5; 5**

The appointed scriptural way to humility is prayer and fasting, bringing our souls to the subjection of God's authority.

ix.   Self-control

Self-Control teaches us to say 'NO' to ungodliness and worldly passions, and to live upright and godly lives in this present age. Why in the present age? We get the answers in **Romans 1; 18-32.** Although we are living in a very dark age, the character of GOD has been made known to every one:

"For *since the creation of the world God's invisible qualities- His eternal power and divine nature- have been clearly seen, being understood from what has been made, so that people are without excuse*

Although they claimed to be wise, they became fools and exchanged the glory of the immortal God for images made to look like a mortal human being and birds and animals and reptiles

Therefore God gave them over in sinful desires of their hearts to sexual impurity for the degrading of their bodies with one another

They exchanged the truth about God for a lie, and worshipped and served created things rather than the creator- who is forever praised Amen

Because of this God gave them over to shameful lusts. Even their women exchanged natural sexual relations for unnatural ones. In the same way men also abandoned natural relations with women and were inflamed with lust for one another. Men committed shameful acts with one another, and received in themselves the due penalty for their error.

Furthermore just as they did not think it worthwhile to retain the knowledge of God, so God gave them over to a depraved mind, so that they do what ought not to be done.

They have become filled with every kind of wickedness, evil, greed and depravity. They are full of envy, murder, strife, deceit, and malice. They are gossips, slanderers, god haters, insolent, arrogant and boastful, they invent evil ways of doing evil, and they disobey their parents

They have no understanding, no fidelity, no love, and no mercy

Jackson Odeny Oyoo;   Memories of my life.

Although they know God's righteous decree that those who do such things deserve death, they not only continue to do these things but also approve those who practice them''

To be in a self-controlled life is the mark of one who has received the grace, a sign that the grace of God is working in one's life.

In the book of Titus chapter 2 there is a clear instruction to this generation. The lord is saying that the grace we have comes with responsibility, and that the church ought to be preparing for the Kingdom of glory. The lord is saying that there is a certain conduct, a certain behavior and practice that goes with the grace that we have received. The lord gives instruction on how we ought to behave in the eyes of the world. We see that the grace has appeared, bringing salvation, teaching and training the church.

So we cannot continue the way we were in the world. **Titus 2 v.12-14**. Tells us that;

*"For the grace of God has appeared that offers salvation to all people. It teaches us to say **NO** to ungodliness and worldly passions, and to live self-controlled, upright and godly lives in this present age, while we wait for the blessed hope-the*

appearing of the glory of our great God and savior, Jesus Christ, who gave himself for us to redeem us from all wickedness and to purify for himself a people who are his own, eager to do what is good"

The Lord was tortured to purchase the grace for me and for everybody, something I did not deserve. I have told my will to submit to the Lordship of Christ. I do the race for a crown that will last eternally, not running aimlessly, not like a boxer fighting the air. No, I strike a blow to my body so that after I have preached to others, I myself will not be disqualified for the price. **1 Corinthians 9; 27.**

My greatest rider is that our attitude; the sum total of our values, knowledge and beliefs, blended with our behaviors; the sum total of our decisions, actions and communication develop into our culture. Let our culture be that of saying NO to ungodliness, leading self-controlled and upright lives as we wait for the blessed hope.

In exercising self-control, the power of the tongue is of greatest importance. Whenever I pray I know that the tongue has tremendous power to affect people and situations either for good or for evil. The following few verses attest to this:

Jackson Odeny Oyoo;   Memories of my life.

- *The words of the reckless pierce like swords, but the tongue of the wise brings healing* **Proverbs 12;18**
- *The soothing tongue is a tree of life, but a perverse tongue crushes the spirit* **Proverbs 15;4**
- *The tongue has the power of life and death, and those who love it eat the fruit of its life* **Proverbs 18;21**
- *The tongue is a small part of the body, but it makes great boasts. Consider what a great forest is set on fire by a small spark. The tongue also is a fire, a world of evil among the parts of the body. It corrupts the whole body, sets the whole course of one's life on fire, and is itself set on fire by hell* **James 3;5-6**
- *With the tongue we praise our Lord and father and with it we curse human beings, who have been made in God's likeness* **James 3; 9-10**

CHAPTER 10

MY FINAL GOAL: Proclaiming salvation to mankind and Submitting to the Lord eternally

After living in this world for almost sixty five years now, I conclude by saying that there are three problems which humanity has failed to solve, thus

1.   Sin
2.   Human suffering
3.   Death

It doesn't matter the technological advances and the computer age we are living in, these problems will always be with us. Humanity will not offer a solution. If humanity had a solution, the richest men who have walked the earth like Henry Ford and Steve Jobs or the greatest world leaders like Nelson Mandela and George Washington would still be alive today. Yet all the rich people and great leaders had portions of their sufferings. Some went through the most unstable families and some went through the cruelest divorces. Their monies could not save them. In the so called advanced

Jackson Odeny Oyoo;   Memories of my life.

societies, there is not a single person without a problem or a worry. The same applies to lesser societies.

What about the regrets at the point of death? I cannot have a clearer example than that of my father on his death bed on 27th April 1963. He talked about the suffering that his children would go through because of his imminent death. He even requested his brothers in law to come to the rescue of his children after his death. I think he never talked about salvation and eternal life.

However, even after getting all the good education during my time, as per the dreams of my father, my life came to naught. I was overtaken with sin, absolute lack, a dysfunctional family and a possibility of even an imminent death and condemnation to hell. So neither education nor money offered me a solution to my sufferings. I even researched through my past generations and found they too lived and had their portions of sufferings with no solutions on hand.

I look at majority of our youth of today and find that they too have their self-destructive habits in the form of dissatisfactions; negative competitions, jealousies, abusing and killing of one another, rebellion; Satisfactions in the delicacies of the flesh; phonography, illicit sex, drug and alcohol abuse etc. They are not alone: I was also there and was only rescued by the Lord. These same young people are also searching all over to fill some voids in their lives; some are searching for solutions as to where they came from and to where they are going. The answers are not in sight, so they end up entrenched further in those addictions and even in committing suicide: The final damnation to hell.

What our Lord said when he was on earth and before he went to heaven is of great significance to the human race. He said, and I will mention only four:

1. **In John 10; 10:** *The thief cometh not, but for to steal, and to kill, and to destroy; I am come that they might have life, and that they might have it more abundantly.*

2. **In Mathews 11.28-29:** *come unto me, all ye that labor and are heavy laden, and I will give you rest. Take my yoke upon you, and learn of me; for I am meek and lowly in heart; and you shall find rest unto your souls.*

Jackson Odeny Oyoo; Memories of my life.

3. **In Luke 24, 46:** Then he said unto them *"This is what is written: The Christ will suffer and rise from the dead on the third day. And repentance and forgiveness of sins will be preached in his name to all nations, beginning at Jerusalem".*

4. **In Acts 1; 8 :***"But you will receive power when the Holy Spirit comes on you; and you will be my witnesses in Jerusalem, and in all Judea and Samaria, and to the ends of the earth"*

I am indeed a witness to what the lord has done to my life when I made the decision to follow him.

The love of God to the human race was expressed through the giving of his begotten son, Jesus Christ that those who believe in him shall have abundant life welling to eternal life. Without the crucifixion of Jesus Christ on the cross salvation would not have reached the gentile world. Through crucifixion the door to salvation was opened to everyone, Jews or Gentiles. The solution to the human race' unsolved problems of sin, suffering and death lies with coming into fellowship with God through the acceptance of Jesus Christ as our personal savior.

Jackson Odeny Oyoo;   Memories of my life.

In the Old Testament God was dealing with his elect with their flesh. Under the new covenant God is dealing with his elect with his spirit. This spirit comes by repenting of our sins, acknowledging Jesus Christ and accepting him as Lord and savior of our lives.

Once one is born again he or she is sealed with the Holy Spirit – **Ephesians 6; 33.** He is no longer a slave to sin but a slave to righteousness. As a born again Christian, he now has boldness to enter the throne room of God and obtain mercy at times of need. And we know that since Jesus Christ was raised from the dead, death no longer has mastery over him, for when he died he died unto sin on the cross, but now is risen by the power of God and lives unto God. He is on the right hand side of God, pleading and waiting for the saints to enter.

In the same way we who accept Jesus into our lives should count ourselves dead to sin but alive to God in Christ Jesus. In the background we ought to know that our bodies are world conscious, our souls self-conscious and our spirit God conscious. Therefore, after being born again we must always walk in the spirit, so that we do not fulfill the lust of the flesh.

Jackson Odeny Oyoo;   Memories of my life.

In conclusion, the only solution available for sin and human suffering is accepting the Lord as savior, living in righteousness and producing the fruits of the Holy Spirit; Love, Joy, Peace, Longsuffering, Gentleness, Goodness, Faith, Meekness and self-control. Against these, there is no law. As for death the Lord has promised eternal life for those who overcome the world. Their bodies will be translated from dishonor to glory, from weakness to power, from "soulish" to "spiritual" and from mortal to immortal. They will live with the Lord forever.

In the end, I like Paul, should be able to **say 'I have fought the good fight. I have finished the race. I have kept the faith'**. 2 Timothy 4; 7.

EPILOGUE

My life history in summary

In brief I was born on 7th August 1956, the second born child of the Late Edward Oyoo Jabuya and the late Mama Jane Anyango Oyoo. Upon my birth I was nicknamed Jayala. Some people also called me Ja Ulumbi or Ja Marenyo, having been named after my father's Teacher friend, the Late Mwalimu Clement Odeny of Gem Ulumbi. I am a stepson of The Late Daniel Akowa, the late Nashon Owuocha and brother to Mrs. Alice Aseda, the late Julius Nyongo, Evans Wilberforce Omondi, the late Israel Ochieng, the late Dickens Otieno, Jenifer Nyamohanga and Nerea Omolo.

Having lost my father at a tender age of seven years in 1963 and because of a poor family background at our Gem Rae home, I and my elder sister Alice were in 1964 taken to our mother's home of birth by our Aunt, the late Joan Akoth Sande. Here we would be brought up by our maternal grandmother, the late Rosa Akanda Majanga, who effectively shaped our early lives through high standards of discipline, hard work and honesty blended with humility.

Jackson Odeny Oyoo;   Memories of my life.

My early life was also shaped through the support of my maternal uncles Hezborn Omolo Majanga and Jeconiah Achola Majanga who ensured that I had the best education.

Faithful to my Uncles commitment and hopes, I did not disappoint them for I went through Nyakoko primary school (1964 – 1970), Miwani secondary school (1971-1974) and Kisii High School (1975-1976), where I would pass final exams with flying colors at every level. This enabled me to secure a chance at Nairobi University from 1977 up to 1980 where I graduated with an honors degree in Business Administration. As bright as I was, my uncles had earlier insisted that I must continue with my education after my fourth form, despite the fact that I had been called to train as a Pilot at a Pilot Training School in Uganda.

Upon my graduation from University, I was offered employment as a supplies Officer in the Ministry of Finance where I served for one year before taking up a job at the then Kenya Posts and Telecommunications Corporation. At Kenya Posts I served in various capacities starting as An Assistant Postal Controller and rising through the ranks to the level of Assistant Regional Postal Manager. After leaving Kenya Posts I did consultancy jobs for some time and later took formal employment as Human Resource Manager at Sondu Miriu Hydro Power Project from 2009 to 2010. After a short stint at Sondu Miriu, I capped formal working life by being engaged as a Commissioner with Kisumu County Public Service Board from 2013 up to 2018. I remain actively engaged by undertaking online consultancies through which I am earning my living.

I was very passionate about education. I believe that it was in education that I was enabled to spring from a hopeless family background to the highest level of academic brilliance during my time and the highest professional competence in the line of duty, capacities which would later earn me a title referred to by friends and foes alike as Commissioner.

The passion for education drove me to pay for the schooling of all my brothers and sisters up to, as I used to say, the highest level where their brains would take them, the highest level of their academic competence. Indeed I moved with them wherever I went in line of duty i.e. Nairobi, Machakos, Garissa and Kisumu. I did this even for my brother's children, Zakayo Onyango and Bernard Ochieng, after their fathers' demise. I knew in my heart that if I did not intervene in their situations nobody would.

Jackson Odeny Oyoo;   Memories of my life.

I always say I am giving back to individuals and the communities which stood with me during my earlier days of struggle, notwithstanding Gem Rae and Kabar Communities which were key in this respect. I have done so with great zeal and passion.

I developed an intense love for our Lord and savior Jesus Christ. In 1998, after a long struggle between evil and good, I surrendered my life to the Lord and thereafter lived a simple life of love, meekness and peace, serving the lord with all my heart. This would endear him to participate in the formation of a Christian group called '*Transformation for Abundance in christ*' and rally my local clan members into the formation of a community based organization called '*JOK'OYOO CBO*'. Here the simple message which I faithfully articulated in my morning prayers was 'Seek ye the Kingdom of God and His righteousness first, and all these things shall be added to you as well' (Mathews 6:33). I still continue doing so.

Of all the experiences in life, there is no other virtue that became more endearing to me than the virtue of unconditional love. I not only embody it but live it with all its eternal attributes of limitless forgiveness to all people who step on my toes. Behind the scenes and unknown to many,

Jackson Odeny Oyoo;   Memories of my life.

this unconditional love virtue has touched people across my neighborhood and within my sub clan JOKOYOO, in such a way that quarrels, infightings, gossips, jealousies, selfishness and all acts bordering on fleshly desires have been swallowed up with the victory of love, peace and unity.

The Lord found me when I was already married to my two wives; Lovena Awuor Oyoo, whom I married in 1981 and Janet Nthambi Odeny, whom I married in 1993. I remain committed to them in equal measure to the end. In all they have borne me seven children, namely: Anita Achieng (1982), Bruno Odhiambo (1985), Wilkister Otieno (1988), Daisy Oyoo (1990), Francis Omondi (1994), Carolyne Atieno (1998) and Peter Onyango (2001). My life has also been graced with two grandchildren; Rama and Isabelle.

I have instilled in all of them the virtue of unconditional love and self-control, bearing with each other's weaknesses. I always pray to the Lord every morning for the blessings of protection upon our lives, something which the lord has faithfully done and will continue to do.

THE END

Jackson Odeny Oyoo;   Memories of my life.

I have shared the memories of my life in two paradigms: one, when I was always struggling with life, exposed to some of the best institutions of learning in my mother country, Kenya. I became an academic giant in my own right during my time but struggled through many ups and downs of life, some so bitter, some so sweet. I travelled places, became exposed to different training institutions and different places of recreation. I met different people, who exposed me to good habits and bad habits. I continued searching and searching for what I called the unknown.

Secondly, the memories have helped me to understand my roots, the value of life and the secret of filling an empty life. They have driven me to stop searching for the unknown and give God the first place in my life in all circumstances, whether good or bad. I only understood the value of life when I went through my most difficult circumstances, the circumstances which helped to shape my life to be what I am today in Christ Jesus. I have no regrets at all of living in the Kingdom of God, and I'll continue to do so, without any fear of contradiction, until I transit from this temporal body I am clothed in, to the inheritance of a higher eternal life which is my hope.

Jackson Odeny Oyoo;   Memories of my life.